T0095421

The Principles of Ethical Youth Coaching

Justin E. Mayer & Dr. John E. Mayer

authorHOUSE®

AuthorHouse™
1663 Liberty Drive
Bloomington, IN 47403
www.authorhouse.com
Phone: 1-800-839-8640

© 2012 Center for Ethical Youth Coaching. All rights reserved.

No part of this book may be reproduced, stored in a retrieval system, or transmitted by any means without the written permission of the author.

Published by AuthorHouse 2/13/2012

ISBN: 978-1-4670-4472-1 (e)
ISBN: 978-1-4670-4473-8 (hc)
ISBN: 978-1-4670-4474-5 (sc)

Library of Congress Control Number: 2011917769

Any people depicted in stock imagery provided by Thinkstock are models, and such images are being used for illustrative purposes only. Certain stock imagery © Thinkstock.

This book is printed on acid-free paper.

Because of the dynamic nature of the Internet, any web addresses or links contained in this book may have changed since publication and may no longer be valid. The views expressed in this work are solely those of the author and do not necessarily reflect the views of the publisher, and the publisher hereby disclaims any responsibility for them.

Contents

Introduction
The Center for Ethical Youth Coaching

Mission Statement:

The mission of the Center for Ethical Youth Coaching is to raise the ethical standards of coaches who work with young athletes, through research, publication, credentialing and public presentations. As a result of raising these ethical standards, young athletes will be in the best possible position to learn and grow through sports. Sports are a tremendous way to learn about life and develop life skills. It is, therefore, important that coaches are prepared to guide young athletes in the most ethical manner possible.

Background:

In June of 2010, the International Sports Professionals Association (ISPA) conducted research on the state of Youth Coaching. ISPA was astounded to find that in youth sports ethics was given far less attention than other areas. The research showed that ethical concerns in youth coaching are mentioned only briefly and at most given one or two paragraphs in youth coaching manuals. After concluding this initial research, ISPA decided to start an exploratory committee on the feasibility of issuing a coaching certification on ethics in youth sports. The exploratory committee concluded that there was a need for such a certification. On October 4, 2010 ISPA began development of the Ethical Youth Coach Certification (EYC). The purpose of the ethical youth coaching certification is not to replace sport-specific coaching training but to complement it by adding consideration of ethics, psychological development, guidance, discipline, motivation, safety, healthy lifestyle practices and parental involvement. The development of this certification also led to the creation of the Center for Ethical

Youth Coaching (CEYC). The Center for Ethical Youth Coaching is a not-for-profit organization. In addition to administering the EYC certification, the CEYC will offer an accreditation for youth sports training businesses and will be a leading advocate for promoting ethics in youth sports.

The aim of the training program contained in these pages is to provide a strong background in ethics and other vital skills listed previously. The program goes beyond the tactics of coaching specific sports, aiming to make the coach more successful and ensure the safety, growth and enjoyment of the players and their parents. The Center for Ethical Youth Coaching defines a youth athlete as high school age and below (18 and under). This manual covers the above issues comprehensively, as the issues raised in this training program are far too important to be presented in one chapter. Developing the ethical side of a player is often neglected, as coaches tend to focus on preparing their players for competition. The Center for Ethical Youth Coaching believes that players must be developed in an environment of ethical practice in order to create the complete player.

Special Note:

As was stated above, this book is designed for athletes 18 and under. However, some of the concepts brought up in this book may apply differently to different age groups. For example, during a team meeting with seven year olds you would not hand out lengthy pamphlets on sportsmanship; you would hand out more age-appropriate material. It is particularly important to recognize that the younger the athlete the more "self centered" ("me stage", they are primarily concerned about what benefits them) they are and thus the principle of "what is good for the team" can be lost on them. Since older players typically have more experience, they may adopt some of the concepts addressed in this book more quickly (the opposite may also be true!). Several chapters specifically discuss strategies for dealing with different age groups. However, the remainder of the book addresses all age groups. It is up to the coach to determine the level of the players' understanding. Furthermore, this book is gender neutral, and is applicable to both males and females.

Another note: while this book is focused on team sports, most of the concepts are easily adapted to "individual" sports.

Preface
The Aim of the Ethical Youth Coach

If you have played sports for an extended period of time you have undoubtedly encountered various coaching styles, some good and some bad. Think back to all the good coaches you have had and use the following lines to write down the qualities you associate with these coaches:

_____

_____

_____

_____

_____

Now write down the qualities you associate with the bad coaches you have had:

_____

_____

_____

_____

_____

_____

The qualities you listed for the good coaches begin to define your image of an ethical coach. Here are some of the qualities an ethical youth coach should possess.

- Acts according to high moral standards
- Trustworthy
- Respects Participants
- Empowers youth
- Treats players equally
- Informed
- Self-aware
- Honest
- Honorable
- Follows a safe training plan

If you had any of these on your list of things that define a good coach then you are on the right track to understanding what makes for an ethical youth coach. In order to define a bad coach take the opposite of the above list, i.e. low moral standards, etc. Your duty as a Certified Ethical Youth Coach will be to not only embody the above principles but also promote them. Below are two examples of coaches, one ethical and one unethical.

Hypothetical models of youth coaches:

The Ethical Coach:

Mary coaches a girl's volleyball team composed of girls age 12-14. Mary always arrives to practice 15 minutes early to finalize the practice schedule. Mary starts off each practice by pointing out the positive aspects of the previous practice and discussing areas that need improvement. Throughout the practice Mary tells each player that they are doing a great job. When the physical part of the practice ends, Mary sits the team down and has them fill out their journals, asking them to write about what they learned in practice. Furthermore, Mary hands out an article about sportsmanship for the players to take home and read. Mary ends the practice by telling everybody they did a great job.

The Unethical Coach:

Joe coaches a boys' little league baseball team with boys ranging in age from 10-12. He routinely shows up 15 minutes late and typically looks frazzled upon arrival. Right when he arrives at practice he starts yelling at the team for their loss in the last game. Joe immediately makes the team run because of this loss. When the team is done running, Joe points out to each player how they "screwed up" in the last game. When the practice ends Joe warns the team that if they do not win the next game they will do even more running at the next practice.

These two examples are meant to give you a starting point in building your definition of an Ethical Youth Coach. The Center for Ethical Youth Coaching defines an ethical youth coach as someone who is concerned about developing the complete player. This includes not only developing the fundamental skills necessary for youth to be successful in their sport but also developing skills that will benefit their daily lives. The purpose of this manual is not to talk about individual sports skills but to talk about the ways in which coaches develop a player's character and life skills. A coach armed with this book and the knowledge to instruct players on the tactical concepts of a particular sport will be able to develop the "complete player." As a coach your goal is to create and foster a learning environment where your players can develop both sports skills and life skills. Remember, you are not coaching professional athletes; you are coaching youth athletes. Many of the ways in which a professional coach treats his or her athletes does not apply to youth coaching. Many coaches try to copy the manner of the professional coach, yet few of those skills directly translate to the youth level. The sole aim of the professional coach is to win; this should not be the case for youth coaches. It is not uncommon to witness at any level, from 7-year-old little league baseball to high school soccer, for the focus to be solely on winning. Coaches who become blindly focused on winning tend to concentrate on developing the sports-specific skills that they perceive will have the greatest immediate impact on their team's success. When this happens the coach neglects developing the complete player. The **complete player** is composed of two primary sides and within each of these sides there are subcomponents. The two sides of the complete player are the **Character Development Side** and the **Sports-Specific Side**. The following chart represents key aspects of the complete player.

The Complete Player

Sports-Specific Side	Character Development Side
Motor skills for given sport	***Sportsmanship***
Conditioning	***Developmental skills*** -*Confidence* -*Maturity* -*Self-esteem* -*Socialization* -*Discipline* -*Responsibility* -*Focus*
Sports Drills	*Translates sports lessons into daily life*
Specific Sports Knowledge	*Student of the game*
	Healthy Lifestyle

-Winning / Losing-
-Teamwork-
(Has impact on both sides)

The purpose of this book is to focus on the right side of the above chart, the character development side. The reason this book is focused on the character development side is because it is often not the focus of coaching resources. Most books dedicate only a small chapter to this very important topic. However, how can you have a complete player if one whole side of their development is ignored or glossed over? The answer is, you can't! The Center for Ethical Youth Coaching aims to put a stop to this neglect and aid coaches in developing the character development side of the player.

In the end the overarching goal of the Ethical Youth Coaching Model is to instill the following **four values in players**:

-Developmental skills
-A healthy lifestyle
-Sportsmanship (ethical treatment of others)
-Teamwork

These values are beneficial not only while young athletes are engaged in sports but also throughout their lives.

Developmental Skills

Every coach wants to have confident individuals on his or her team. Confidence is one of the key developmental skills that sports imparts to its participants. A **confident player** is one who believes in their ability to achieve a goal. The greatest athletes in history all have one thing in common: confidence. Confident players, at times, can seem capable of achieving anything. Confidence does not just have benefits in the athletic realm; its benefits permeate every area of a person's life. A confident student performs better and a confident businessman is better able to excel at his or her job. Athletes who learn to be confident in their abilities on the playing field are able to apply this confidence to their everyday lives. However, as was previously pointed out, mere participation in sports does not guarantee that individuals will gain confidence elsewhere in their lives. The Ethical Youth Coaching Model provides a framework to enable coaches to instill this confidence in their players. For many, confidence is not something that is immediately achieved. The best way to build confidence is through a gradual approach.

In addition to confidence there are several other key developmental skills that are impacted by sports participation. Players who participate in sports tend to display higher levels of **maturity**; often this is a product of a coach who facilitates mature behavior on the team. One of the "side effects" of participation in sports is increased **self-esteem** (this will be discussed more in depth in Chapter 12). Children who play sports interact with other children for extended periods of time. This interaction often leads to increased socialization skills. A good sports team has rules and an EYC coach enforces those rules. It is through these rules that players learn discipline. A youth athlete learns the value of being responsible through their participation in sports. Goal setting is important to the EYC coach. Players on such a coach's team are made aware of the goals they have for the day, week, month and season, and then they pursue these goals. Step by step they achieve them. It is through this gradual approach that they learn the importance of dedication and focus in achieving goals.

Healthy Lifestyle

With the incidence of obesity reaching epidemic proportions in the United States, the importance of promoting a healthy lifestyle is critical. One of the greatest services a coach can provide is to instill in their young players healthy habits that they will carry with them for the rest of their lives. Sadly, the exact opposite often happens. By using unethical or negative techniques some coaches create an environment that turns young people away from adopting a healthy lifestyle. The EYC coach seeks to put an end to these poor health habits and produce responsible athletes who care for their bodies. The Ethical Youth Coach is not solely concerned about the moment, the game, or the season; they are dedicated to the healthy lifestyle of the person.

Sportsmanship

Teaching players how to honor their opponent is not only an integral part of their participation, but also teaches them how to deal with people they encounter on an everyday basis. A coach who teaches his or her players how to treat opponents with respect instills in them values that will benefit their lifelong interactions with others.

Teamwork

Undoubtedly most of your players will go on to work in jobs that involve communicating and working with other individuals. The sprit of team unity that you teach them will allow them to work more effectively with people throughout their lives. The ability to work well with others is a critical skill that has a lasting impact on your players.

Why Ethics?

The question some coaches might bring to the table is, why should they be concerned about developing the character development side of the player? Shouldn't the players' parents instill these values in their children? Shouldn't coaches just stick to teaching players about sports?

A coach should be concerned about developing the character development side of the player because they are in a unique position, as the child's coach, to use sports as a vehicle for teaching them life lessons. By developing the complete player, you are not only teaching your players to play a sport better, but also teaching them life lessons. They will carry these enriching life lessons with them through the rest of their lives. Very few athletes are able to make a career of sports. However, anyone who has ever stepped foot on a playing field can benefit from participating. Following the Ethical Youth Coaching Model will help coaches develop the character development side of the player.

The layout of this book

The overall aim of this book is to teach coaches, or for that matter parents, about **the Ethical Youth Coaching Model**. The book is divided into three sections. Section one talks about some basic issues that will help prepare coaches for the five stages of player development. For the most part, this first section talks in a more general sense and lays a foundation for what follows. The second section discusses the five stages of player development. The third section addresses special concerns and issues. Throughout the book the phrase **Ethical Youth Coaching Model** will be used to reference our overall methodology. At the end of each chapter you will find a list of keywords and questions. These are meant to reinforce key points in the chapter and also prepare those who are taking the Ethical Youth Coaching Certification Exam. This book should not be viewed as an end, but rather a beginning. The time to start raising the ethical standards of youth coaching is now! The goal of developing the complete player begins with you.

Keywords:
Complete Player
Character Development Side
Sports-Specific Side
Ethical Youth Coaching Model

Questions:
1) List three qualities of an ethical youth coach.
2) How does the Center for Ethical Youth Coaching define an EYC coach?
3) Describe how you implement ethical practices in your coaching.
4) What are some areas you can work on to become a more ethical coach?
5) Why do coaches oftentimes neglect the ethical side of player development?
6) What is the purpose of the EYC coaching model?
7) What is the sole aim of a professional coach?
8) List and describe three key subcomponents of the ethical side of the whole player.
9) List three developmental skills that the EYC coach seeks to develop in their players.
10) As a coach why should you be concerned with developing the complete player?
11) Why should an EYC coach be concerned about promoting a healthy lifestyle?

Suggested Activities:
1) Come up with a list of qualities that define an Ethical Youth Coach. Print them out and place them in a visible spot where you can see them every day.

Part I

The Ethical Youth Coaching Model

Chapter 1
Positive Coaching

Nothing can stop the person with the right mental attitude from achieving his goal; nothing on earth can help the person with the wrong mental attitude.
-Thomas Jefferson

If you are not committed to following the ideals set forth in this first chapter, there is no reason to read the rest of the book. This may be a bold statement, but the attitude with which you approach your coaching is critical. In this chapter we will discuss the **Positive Coaching Model**. If you follow these suggestions you will ensure that you are reinforcing positive attitudes in your players and creating an environment that will help your players best absorb the EYC model. The positive coaching model ensures that you are always maintaining a positive mental state and encouraging your players. You must always keep in mind that participation in sports for young athletes is not primarily about winning, but about having fun and developing good habits. The concept of winning and losing should be introduced with an emphasis on the positive aspects of each. When the team wins, highlight the aspects that brought about the victory, i.e. dedication to practice. When the team loses, point out the things that were positive about the team's performance. Discuss with the team how they can improve certain areas of their play and how this will enhance their chances of winning in the future. "Keep it positive" should be your mantra! Later in this book we will discuss specific strategies for dealing with the concept of winning.

All too often coaches focus on the record of their team or on individual stats. This is best highlighted by the stat-driven game of baseball. A Little League coach who constantly focuses on players' batting averages is doing little to foster positive attitudes on his or her team. Of course, players with high batting averages will feel great. However, those with less than stellar averages will feel inferior. While highlighting players' stats can be a great way to motivate players, it should be done in moderation. Your players are not playing for million dollar contracts. Your focus should be on overall improvement and not arbitrary stats. If you are coaching children seven and under it is advised not to include any stats in the information you give your players. The key is **moderation**. The first words you say to your players should never be stat-oriented.

The following are some general guidelines to keep in mind in order to ensure that you are following the positive coaching model. Always make sure you are using **"please" and "thank you."** If you need something during practice say "please" and when it is delivered make sure you say "thank you." Make sure all your players are also following your lead and using these two magical words. If you witness a player demanding something of another player immediately address the issue by pointing out that "on this team we say please and thank you." It is very easy to get in the cycle of demanding things on sports teams, particularly when the competitive juices are flowing. Slow down and make please and thank you a habit. It is simple, yet powerful. Thank you.

Always **focus on the positive**. If a player makes an error, deliver the corrective lesson by leading with what the player did correctly. If you are having difficulty finding something positive to say about a given error focus on the player's attitude or approach, then go on to the problem. All too often coaches only use phrases like "you screwed up" rather than addressing why the player "screwed up." Then the coach makes the player repeat the activity that he or she made the error on. There is no problem-solving or instruction in this scenario. Rather than creating this **negative cycle**, make sure you problem-solve about what caused the error to happen. This is not to say that you have to stop the whole practice and spend several minutes addressing what may be a minor issue. The key is to make sure you do not repetitively engage a player in an activity that he or she is struggling with until you address why the player is struggling and how the problem is going to be corrected. This can be as simple as saying "follow the ball more" and then hitting him or her the ball.

The following is a list of ways you can be a positive coach. We encourage you to add to this list.

- Compliment a good play.
- Always lead with a positive statement.
- Have a special snack for the players as a reward for all their hard work.
- Smile.
- Emphasize having fun.
- Practice the drills with the players and while doing so emphasize how much fun you are having.
- Use please and thank you.

Challenges to Your Positive Attitude

Sometimes even the most positive coaches with the most well-planned practice can have a day when the players are not responding and are down on themselves. In these situations it may be best to focus on something that you know the team does well in order to build up the team's confidence. There are also days when the team is having discipline issues, and they are loud, being silly, or not listening. In these instances it may be appropriate to elevate your voice. However, make sure you are keeping your voice under control and not yelling. A great technique to get the team's attention is to stop the practice. In cases where a player's safety is jeopardized it is very important that you act very firmly. You must strongly convey to the team that this type of behavior is not tolerated. Raising your voice may be appropriate when another player's actions are making practice unsafe for other players. Again, stopping practice or removing the misbehaving player from that day's practice is as effective as a raised voice.

Yelling is something that should never enter a coach's tool-kit. The only time we advise raising your voice is to be heard clearly and immediately, such as when the safety of your players is in jeopardy or when extreme disrespect is displayed. For example, if a little league player is wildly swinging a bat near other players it would be appropriate to raise your voice when telling this player to stop.

Furthermore, if a player is taunting another player and using physical force it would be appropriate to raise your voice at the aggressive player so they hear you clearly. It is not appropriate to raise your voice at a player because he or she failed to score or made an error or mistake. Use your judgment when it comes to raising your voice, but remember it is never appropriate to use inappropriate language in the presence of your team. Later in this book we will return to the topic of yelling.

Running as a punishment is never acceptable. The obvious dangers of running as a punishment are that it could overexert your players and cause some serious health issues. Furthermore, when you use running as a punishment you are creating a negative correlation with running. No longer will players see running as a fun activity that is critical to developing their cardiovascular system; running will be seen as a punishment. One of the focuses of an EYC coach is to promote a healthy lifestyle. Making running a punishment runs counter to this goal.

Think About Who you are as a Coach

Another important aspect of positive coaching is to make sure you are focused on the practice or game. What does this mean? Keep the use of your cell phone to a minimum. There is no quicker way to show your players that you are not interested in their success than by constantly talking and texting during practice. Young athletes are continually watching your actions. If you act disinterested, they will become exactly that. Many coaches are quite busy and there are times when taking a call or sending an e-mail is unavoidable. This is understandable. Just make sure that anytime you use your cell phone it is for a good reason and not just to see what your friends are up to.

Try your hardest to eat before practice. Coaches are busy people, and youth coaches are particularly busy because they typically have another job. Sometimes eating gets lost in the shuffle. Don't use practice time or game time to catch up on a meal. Coaches who eat meals during practice are distracted. How would you feel if you went to a coaching seminar only to have the teacher eating a sub sandwich the whole time? Some coaches will even eat during games! If you simply do not have time to eat before practice then make sure your eating is discrete and not a distraction. Always make an honest effort to eat before practices and games.

Another distraction to avoid is talking to people outside the team, i.e. with friends. It is not respectful to be distracting the team from practice because you are chatting on the sideline with a friend. Save the socializing for after practice.

While this book does not focus on the sports-specific side of coaching, the important topic of pushing players too hard and too soon will be brought up frequently. An Ethical Youth Coach must be committed to a gradual training plan that progressively builds their players' conditioning and not to have their players practice to the point of exhaustion. As an EYC coach you must put an end to this dangerous practice. An EYC coach knows the limits of his or her players and always operates within those limits.

Finally, a reminder: the attitude you bring to each and every practice is critical for the success of implementing the Ethical Youth Coaching Model. A coach who comes to practice in a sour mood will be unable to successfully utilize the strategies outlined in the forthcoming chapters no matter how noble his or her intentions. It is no fun to learn from a teacher who has a bad attitude. When you are with your team smile and be positive.

Key Words and Concepts:
The Positive Coaching Model
Please and Thank You
Focus on the Positive
Negative Cycle

Questions:
1) List several ways you can be positive during your team's practice.
2) Why should a coach always utilize the positive coaching model?
3) What should a coach focus on when his or her team loses?

4) Why is running as punishment never acceptable in youth sports?
5) Why should a coach **not** focus on stats?
6) (True or False) It is okay for the first thing you say to a player to be stat-oriented.
7) What should a coach do when his or her team is not responding during a practice?
8) (True or False) It is okay to have yelling in your coaching tool-kit.
9) Why is eating during practice not acceptable?
10) Why is the attitude you bring to practices or games important to the success of implementing the EYC model?

Activities:

1) Create your own list of Positive Coaching characteristics.

Chapter 2
The Ethical Youth Coach

While it is up to each individual coach to develop his or her own style and system there are several qualities and characteristics that all EYC coaches possess. This chapter will talk about the qualities that are critical to your success as an EYC coach. One quality that you will find missing from this list is experience. While experience will certainly make you a better coach, particularly when this experience is directed towards a positive coaching style, it is not essential for being a good youth coach. Many youth coaches are "first timers" and to tell someone they can't be a good coach because they don't have experience would be counter to what The Center for Ethical Youth Coaching promotes. Remember, youth coaching is very different from coaching professional sports. Criticism targeted at inexperienced, first-time professional coaches does not apply to youth coaches.

Here is a list of essential qualities an EYC coach possesses. We call this the **EYC Coach Checklist**. Whenever you find yourself in doubt go through this checklist to ensure that you are on the right path.

EYC Coach Checklist
-Passionate
-Committed
-Organized
-Knowledgeable about the sport you are coaching (always improving your skills/ always learning)
-Communicates Effectively
    -Verbally
    -Physically (Body Language)
-Responsible

-Has a Coaching Philosophy

Passionate

Let's be honest, if you do not have a passion for coaching youth sports it will be incredibly difficult to be a good coach. Whether you are a school coach or a volunteer, your passion is the fuel that keeps you going as a coach. Ask yourself this simple question: why am I coaching youth sports? If something along the lines of "Because I love helping children succeed" does not pop into your head then you may want to reconsider coaching. If your motivation is money or winning at all costs you are certainly in the wrong line of work. However, if you have a passion for coaching youth sports and truly want to help children, then you have the most important characteristic of an EYC coach. Whenever coaching gets difficult, look back to the passion that inspired you to coach. Your coaching truly provides a great service to society and you should be proud of what you do.

Committed

While quite often passion is followed up by commitment there are many cases in which this is not true. Some coaches have tremendous passion but lack the commitment necessary to be a good coach, and vice versa. Coaching youth sports requires a lot of time and energy, and if you are not committed it will be impossible to be a good coach. Commitment does not just mean showing up to practice on time and never canceling a practice. A committed coach is one who takes it upon himself or herself to develop the complete player. A committed coach goes out of their way to help players and help youth sports in general. Being a committed coach does not mean you have to spend every waking hour dedicated to coaching. However, if you are not willing to dedicate time to coaching outside of practice and games, then you should reevaluate your commitment to coaching. Most coaches have numerous responsibilities other than coaching; therefore, the next key characteristic of a coach is crucial.

Organized

Chances are that youth coaching is not your primary job. In fact, most youth coaches are volunteers who have a full time job, and a family. By definition, your time is very limited. It would be a shame to waste the limited amount of time you have with the team reorganizing your coaching-related materials because they were haphazardly organized the first time. It is vitally important that you keep your coaching materials well-organized in order to stay on top of your game as a coach. We strongly suggest that you keep coaching folders or files. Start by filling these folders with tips you get from this book. Label each folder individually, and make sure these folders are easy to access, whether they are physical or virtual. In the next chapter we will talk about how to create a practice plan. Make sure you have a folder dedicated to your practice plans, and if your handwriting is not easily legible make sure you type out the practice plan for easy reference. If you are not using a calendar to organize your life, please get one for your coaching and write down all relevant dates. A little bit of organization goes a long way and it is vital to maximizing your effectiveness as a youth coach.

Knowledgeable about Sport Coaching and Athletics

As an EYC coach it is important to have knowledge about the sport you are coaching and understand the basics of athletic training. Further, you should always keep a mindset of continually increasing your knowledge of the sport and the needs of the players. It is important to draw a distinction between knowledge of a sport and mastery of a sport. Someone who has knowledge of a sport understands the basics, i.e. how to swing a bat, what each position does, the rules of the game, etc. Someone who has mastery of a sport understands intricate strategies and advanced concepts, i.e. how airflow affects the path of a soccer ball. To be an EYC coach you must have knowledge of the sport you are coaching, but you do not have to be a master. If you are a first-time coach, see the resources section in Appendix C for where to find important information on the "X's and O's" of the sports you are about to coach. Furthermore, it is important that first time coaches seek the guidance of experienced coaches. If you are unsure in your knowledge of the sport you are coaching look over the materials you have compiled and talk to a fellow coach to gain more insight. If you have been coaching for a while make sure you have not become complacent and always seek to gain more knowledge about the sport you are coaching. Whatever your experience level as a coach, do not be afraid to seek the help of others if you are unsure about something. Moreover, don't teach your players something that you are unsure of simply to avoid admitting you don't actually know it. As a youth coach it is okay if you do not know something; you are not a professional coach who has a contract riding on his or her understanding of all aspects of the game. You actually provide a great model for young people when you admit that you don't know everything, but will try hard to find answers.

In addition to understanding the basics of the sport you are coaching it is also important to have an understanding of physiology and athletic training. The next chapter will touch upon how to set up safe practices. The chapter on Special Situations and First Aid will also touch upon several physiology-related issues. See also the resource section (Appendix C) for ways to gain further knowledge in this area. Like your sports knowledge, a mastery of all things related to athletic conditioning is not needed. However, understanding the basics is critical for the safety of your players.

Communicates Effectively

A coach could have all the passion and knowledge in the world but if they are not able to communicate this passion and knowledge they will be ineffective coaches. In order to be a good coach you do not need to be a master orator; all you need is to be an effective communicator. This section will offer some advice to get you started. The rest of the book will frequently address how to be an effective communicator.

First, it is important to understand that coaches communicate both verbally and non-verbally. Verbal communication occurs when a coach speaks to his or her team. Non-verbal communication occurs through a coach's body language and facial expressions. Both can be very powerful sources of communication. Most coaches understand the effects their spoken words can have on their players. However, many coaches ignore the effects that their body language have on their team. Children – even the very young – are quite observant and are looking to you, the coach, as a role model. A coach who is perpetually frowning and slouching will convey to the players that they are not happy and this attitude will often carry over to the players. Conversely, a coach who smiles will put players at ease and allow them to perform at their best. Here are some things to keep in mind about your body language.

Things to do:
-Smile
-Pay Attention
-Stand Tall (not chest pumping tall)
-Keep arms relaxed and at your side
-Make eye contact
-Be energetic and enthusiastic

Things not to do:
-Frown
-Look angry (i.e. flare up nostrils)
-Point (when not appropriate)
-Walk lazily (coaches love to do this)
-Look stunned when a player does something wrong
-Act out an aggressive gesture (i.e. kicking at the air)
-Use profane language
-Yell

By following the above advice and other examples throughout this book, a coach will be assured that his or her body language is creating a positive environment for their team. Remember, as a coach it is important to be aware of all your actions, including body language.

Like non-verbal communication, verbal communication has a tremendous impact on your team. A coach's words can inspire a team to achieve things they didn't think were possible. The opposite is also true – a coach's words can deflate the sprits of players and in some cases turn a player away from sports. With all this weight riding on a coach's words the question becomes, what should a coach say and how should he or she speak to his or her team? The good news is that as long as you follow your passion and adhere to the principles of an EYC coach you should have no problem communicating with your team. One key component of communicating effectively is to be prepared for every practice and game. A coach who is unprepared will fumble for the right words and speak in circles. In the next chapter we will show you how to set up a practice plan. Before each practice, review your practice plan and make sure you are ready to execute this plan. Even at the youngest levels it is important that you keep your communications with your team professional. Please and thank you (as discussed in chapter one) should be commonplace on your team and everyone should refer to each other in a respectful manner. Nicknames are a great way to have fun; just make sure these names are respectful and not degrading. Just because a player goes along with a nickname does not mean he or she likes being called "Slow Joe" or "Lazy Susan."

Another important element to consider is the age group you are coaching. A high school coach is able to communicate in a much more sophisticated manner than someone coaching seven year-olds. Furthermore, the length of communication should vary based on the age group you are coaching. Younger children need a lot more stimulus than older children. A seven year-old will have a hard time sitting through a lecture on how to swing a bat without actually attempting to swing the bat. When dealing with younger children it is also important to remember that much of their actions are focused on themselves. This is called the "me stage of development." For younger players (5-7) it is best to highlight individual achievements, yet still emphasizing the role of the team as often as possible. As you mature as a coach you will develop your abilities to communicate to your team. The most important thing to remember is to be prepared for every practice and game and always communicate to your players with respect.

Responsible

This characteristic may seem like common sense to most coaches, which is a good thing. However, in numerous observational studies conducted by International Sports Professionals Association it became clear that while most coaches recognize responsibility as a key characteristic of a coach, some do not live this principle. Arriving late, canceling practice, being unprepared, dressing improperly and poor hygiene are just some of the irresponsible behaviors we've observed. An EYC coach always acts in a responsible manner and would never exhibit the above behavior. Show up on time and take pride in your appearance. If you are constantly late and dressed improperly your players will begin to mirror your actions. Remember that your body language speaks to kids. If you look sloppy at practice, you are screaming, "I don't care!"

An EYC coach is not only responsible for his or her team but also for promoting ethical principles in sports in general, and more specifically the league in which they coach. If you see another coach violating the code of conduct set forth by the league and/or the EYC code of conduct, it is your duty to report these violations to the proper individuals. It is important to intervene immediately if you ever witness a coach jeopardizing the safety of his or her players. If you witness a coach teaching a technique that you do not agree with (and this technique is safe) it is not appropriate to immediately intervene. The best thing to do in this situation is to approach the coach when he or she is away from his or her team and respectfully offer an alternative technique, making sure that you have a strong explanation for why your method is preferable. Simply going up to a coach and telling them that the way they coach is wrong will only create hostility. Undoubtedly throughout your coaching career there will be numerous instances where you can offer unsolicited advice to other coaches, but make sure you have a plan for offering this advice in the most respectful manner.

Coaching Philosophy

As an EYC coach your coaching philosophy should be strongly rooted in ethics and the aim of your philosophy is to develop the complete player. Use the principles set forth in this book as a guide in developing your coaching philosophy. Coaching philosophy is something that a coach develops over time and is something that is continually evolving as coaches are immersed in different situations. One of the major tenets of the CEYC is that a coach is always learning. It is through this learning that a coach refines their coaching philosophy. By choosing to become an EYC coach you have taken a great step in developing a coaching philosophy that will help promote the best qualities in youth athletes. One of the most important steps you can take in developing a coaching philosophy is to be thoughtful about all aspects of the sport you coach. Be a student of the game. Always try to learn from other coaches and never pass up an opportunity to hear thoughtful feedback. Never pass up an opportunity to attend useful coaching seminars. If you have not already started a coaching library, start one (this is another good folder to keep). A coach who thinks he or she knows everything about the sport they are coaching is destined for failure. Every day you step onto the playing field, open a book or attend a seminar so that you are learning something about coaching. Combine this knowledge with principles learned from the EYC program and you will have a coaching philosophy that is unique to you. With this coaching philosophy you will be able to positively impact the lives of all your players. Your coaching philosophy will develop naturally. Don't stress out if you are unable to immediately identify your coaching philosophy.

An EYC coach seeks to embody the above characteristics. However, an EYC coach also recognizes that they will make mistakes along the way. Learn from your mistakes and always strive to embody the above characteristics. If you fall short of embodying any of the above characteristics, don't panic, just commit yourself to improving.

Keywords:
-EYC Coach Checklist
-Passionate
-Committed
-Organized
-Knowledgeable
-Communicates Effectively
-Responsible
-Coaching Philosophy

Questions:
1) List three qualities from the EYC coach checklist.
2) Why is passion so important in coaching?
3) (True or False) A committed coach always has passion.
4) Explain the difference between knowledge of a sport and mastery of a sport.

5) (True or False) As an EYC coach you must have a mastery of the sport(s) you are coaching.
6) (True or False) It is important to seek the guidance of other coaches.
7) Can a coach who is a horrible communicator be an effective coach? Why or why not?
8) Describe the role non-verbal-communication in coaching.
9) List three things you should be doing to promote positive body language.
10) What is one of the key components of being an effective communicator?
11) How does a coach refine his or her coaching philosophy?

Activities:
1) Write down your good qualities as a coach and then write down what you need to work on (use the characteristics in this chapter as a guide).
2) Print out the EYC Coach Checklist and keep it close by for reference.
3) Create your own coaching folders/ files.

Chapter 3
Practice and Game Plans

This chapter focuses more on the nuts and bolts of coaching, and in particular offers guidance to coaches on how to develop practice plans and game plans. One of the most important things you can have for practices and games is a plan, rather than going into either situation blind. Let's first examine how to formulate a practice plan. The following is a sample practice plan that can act as your template when designing your team's practice plan.

Tigers Baseball Team Practice Plan

Date: <u>6/22/2011</u>   Practice Time: <u>1:00-3:15pm</u>

Location: <u>Jefferson Park District field #2</u>

Weather Conditions: <u>Sunny, 85</u>

Practice Goal: **To respond faster in defensive situations.**

Weekly Goal: **To win game against Blue Jays.**

Season Goal: **To win championship.**

Team meeting: 1:00

-Distribute and discuss practice plan. Discuss practice goals and address weekly goal.

-Recap last game.

Warm-Up: 1:15

-5 Minutes light jogging

-Dynamic warm-up drills

-Stretching

Practice Focus #1: 1:30

-Outfield works on going back on fly balls with Coach Dave

-Infield and pitchers work on bent defense with Coach Steve

Hydrate 5 minutes

Practice Focus #2: 2:05

-Whole-team batting practice with Coach Dave and Steve.

Hydrate 5 minutes

Practice Focus #3: 3:05

-Whole-team defensive situations.

Practice Recap: 3:35

-Address issues from practice.

-Players fill out practice log (12 & above)

Player Log (12 & above):

_____

_____

_____

_____

The above has all the basic elements of a good practice plan. However, it is up to each individual coach to tailor the practice to meet his or her team's needs. Notice the built-in hydration breaks; it is very important that you emphasize proper hydration on your team. We will further discuss hydration later in this book. At the bottom of the plan there is space for players to write. The player log serves as a way for players to track their improvement over the course of a season. It is recommended that coaches only have players twelve and older fill out the player log. Players twelve and under should be concerned about building the fundamentals of the sport they are playing, and in any case they often lack the maturity to take an activity such as keeping a log seriously. At the beginning of the season a great idea is to direct your players, twelve and older, to buy a three-ringed binder in which to keep practice plans and game plans, plus any other relevant materials. Keeping a practice binder is a great way to teach your players the importance of tracking their progress and staying organized.

In the above sample log only four lines are included. This is done to encourage players to be short and to the point in their comments; it should only take five minutes for your players to fill in the log. You should encourage them to write how they felt during practice, what they did well, and what they need to work on. It is important that you make this a simple procedure for your players and not a chore. By having them put their comments directly on the practice plans and game plans you are already providing them with all the background information. Make sure the practice plans and game plans are already punched so that players can put them right into their binder. Having your players become proactive in their sports regime is a great way for them to learn how to effectively improve their performance. Furthermore, by reflecting on how they feel during each practice they will be better able to stay in tune with their bodies.

You should also create game plans and, as with practice plans, distribute them to players twelve and older. The following is a sample game plan. Like the sample practice plan, this acts as a template. It is up to you to tailor the plan to your team's needs.

Tigers Baseball Team Game Plan

Date: <u>6/23/2011</u>   **Game Time:** <u>1:00 pm</u>

Location: <u>Jefferson Park District field #2</u>

Weather Conditions: <u>Sunny, 90</u>

Opposing Team: Blue Jays (8-2)

Game Goal: To execute the defensive situations worked on in previous practice.

Opening Lineup (1-3):

A, B, C, D, E, F, G, H, I

Alternate Lineup #1 (4-5)

A, B, C, D, E, F, L, M, N (In actual Plan will be left blank and filled in during game)

Alternate Lineup#2 (5-6)

A, B, C, E, J, K, L, M, N (In actual Plan will be left blank and filled in during game)

Final Score: #######

Player Log:

Position(s) played: _____

_____

_____

_____

_____

A few notes about the above game plan. The letters under the lineups represent players' names. The terms **opening lineup** and **alternate lineup** are used to convey less entitlement than the traditional terms "starting lineup" (aka starters) and "bench lineup" (aka bench players). The lineups are determined using a concept called the winning factor; this concept will be discussed later in great detail. After the game have players (twelve and older) fill out the game plan and put them in their binders. Game plans, like practice plans, are a great way for players to track their progress and take a serious attitude about their sport.

A coach should always create game plans and, when age-appropriate (for kids twelve and older), distribute them to their players. In addition to getting players more involved with the sport they are playing, the above methods teach children organizational skills and how to gain insight into their athletic training. It is important for the coach to make the process of filling out practice and game logs as simple and fun as possible. Playing sports should be fun. It would be a great disservice to your players if you turned this exercise into "homework."

Even the most well-designed practice plan or game plan can be subject to revision when the circumstances call for it. Weather is the most common reason for altering a practice or a game. If severe weather is imminent it is always recommended to cancel practice regardless of whether this practice is outdoors or indoors. Having players drive to an indoor practice in severe weather is never a good idea. However, if the weather is inclement but not severe, attempt to hold the practice indoors if there are available facilities. If the weather turns severe during a practice or game always have a plan in place. Once the weather turns severe have your players follow you to the nearest indoor building to seek shelter until the storm passes or, in the event the game or practice is canceled, a parent picks up the player. If the situation involves a tornado go to the nearest basement or secure building (remember door frames offer the most support in situations where there is no underground or secure shelter). If lightning is spotted stop play immediately, seek shelter and follow league guidelines in resuming play (typically thirty minutes after last sighting). You must stay with your players until a parent or guardian picks them up; never lose sight of your players in weather-related situations. It is imperative that you know where to seek shelter when the weather turns severe (typically this will be the main league field house).

Keywords:
Practice Plan
Game Plan

Questions:
1) What is one of the most important things you can have for practices and games?
2) How old should players be before they fill out player logs?
3) (True or False) Players should spend no more then five minutes filling out player logs.

4) What is one of the most common reasons for altering a practice plan?
5) (True or False) If the weather is **severe** it is okay to hold an indoor practice.

Activities:

1) Create your own practice plans and game plans.

Part II
The Five Stages of Player Development

Chapter 4
The Five Stages of Player Development: An Overview

Let's be honest – very few young athletes will make it to the upper echelons of sports. Out of the estimated one million high school football players in the United States, one hundred and fifty will make it to the NFL. Out of the five hundred and fifty thousand high school basketball players in the United States, fifty will make it to the NBA. Therefore, many people say the most valuable goal of participation in sports is character development. While this sentiment can be true, it is not guaranteed by simple participation. Studies have shown that participating in sports does not ensure that an individual will develop skills that will enhance their character (Rudd & Stoll, 1997). The coach must guide young athletes to receive the valuable life lessons that sports can provide. This is the very reason for the creation of the Ethical Youth Coaching Model. With the Ethical Youth Coaching Model coaches will be able to effectively guide these young athletes to receive the life lessons that sports can teach.

Studies have shown that 73% of boys and 85% of girls believe that a coach should be more concerned about developing character and teaching life skills than winning (Orno, 2010). Clearly our young athletes understand the importance of developing character. However, studies have shown that players are being asked, at an alarming rate, to do unethical things. In a survey conducted by the Josephson Institute, 43% of boys have been taught by their basketball coach how to do illegal moves that are hard to detect (Orno, 2010). The message this sends to our young athletes is clear: it is ok to cheat in order to gain a competitive edge. This is a model that they could potentially take with them for the rest of their lives. We must eradicate these dangerous practices and coach our young athletes in accordance with the highest ethical standards.

At the heart of the Ethical Youth Coaching Model are the **Five Stages of Player Development**. The five stages of player development serve as the blueprint for how coaches can effectively implement the key concepts of the Ethical Youth Coaching Model. The five stages should be followed in order. However, once you complete a stage you do not abandon the concepts and principles in the previous stage. Proceeding through the five stages of player development can be likened to building a stadium. Once the frame is built it is not abandoned; it is actually the foundation for everything else to come. To further the analogy, once the stadium is "complete" it does not merely exist; it must be constantly maintained and improved. Once your players have their "stadium" it is not simply left alone and taken for granted. There are always refinements to be made.

Below is a list of the Ethical Youth Coach's five stages of player development, followed by a brief description of each step.

1) Laying the Foundation (Pre-Season Meeting)
2) Building the Frame (Practices 1-5)
3) Exterior Finishes (Practice 5 – First Game)
4) Working on the Interior (First Game – Last Game)
5) Laying the Field (Last Game – End of Season Party)

Stage One: Laying the Foundation

Without a strong foundation a structure will collapse. If a stadium's foundation is laid too fast and haphazardly the effects can be devastating. The same is true of our young athletes. If a coach neglects to instill a strong ethical foundation in his or her players the effects could be devastating for their development. It is important right from the beginning to address the importance of ethics to your team. The term "ethics" may be one that your players, particularly young players, have never heard, but it is important that you introduce them to it. For an EYC coach, player development begins right from the first time you meet your team.

Stage Two: Building the Frame

Now that we have laid the foundation, it's time to start building the frame. **Building the frame** starts as soon as your players step foot on the playing field. During your first practice you should recall the adage "Rome was not built in a day." It can be particularly frustrating for a coach when dealing with a new group of inexperienced young athletes. These coaches perfectly understand the true meaning of chaos! During such times it is important to practice **positive inner speech**; this is the inner monologue in which you continually remind yourself that *"Rome was not built in a day."* At this stage in the game you are simply interested in building the frame of your team. What does this entail? For starters, put all your players at ease. Many of your players may be full of anxiety, and a fun activity may be just the cure. Make sure all the players introduce themselves so that everyone on the team can become familiar with one another.

It is important that while you are building the frame the intensity of the practices is not too high. If the practices are too vigorous, players' focus will be on the effort required to participate in the practices and not on establishing good habits. Ideally you would spend 4-5 practices building the frame. However, time constraints may not make this possible. Make sure you spend at least two practices building the frame. Remember, the focus during this stage is to develop team cohesion and put the players at ease. The focus should not be on intensity!

Stage Three: Exterior Finishes

Once you are done building the frame it is time to start the **exterior finishes.** Now is when the practices start to ramp up! At this stage you are working on the aerobic conditioning of your players and fully immersing them in drills to improve their skills. Later on we will talk about the many different skills needed to effectively lead these practices. However, never forget to always set a positive tone during every practice and always follow the positive coaching model.

Stages Four and Five both occur during games. These are the stages that are subject to the most change; you will always be making adjustments, as it is impossible to predict how a season will unfold. Remember, if your foundation, frame and exterior are poorly constructed the chances of having a sound structure are zero.

Stage Four: Working on the Interior

Stage Four, **Working on the Interior,** happens both at practice and during games. At this stage you are making sure every player on your team is respectful towards their opponents and the officials. If a player fails to achieve a desired result, focus on how he or she can improve, and aim to achieve the desired result next time. Always focus on the positive. When a player is discouraged, focus on ways to pick him or her up. During this stage it is very important to make sure you convey a positive image to your players. This stage is subject to the most change. You never truly complete this stage; much like being a homeowner there are always things you can work on. If you leave something undone for too long it causes damage to the house. This principle also applies to the individuals you coach. A coach must always be vigilant in responding to his or her players' needs. When a problem is not addressed it affects not only the player but the whole team.

Stage Five: Laying the Field

Laying the Field occurs at the end of the season. This is the reward for all your hard work as a coach! When you look at your players at this stage, you see individuals who are more confident, treat each other with respect and are able to carry the lessons they have learned from playing sports into their daily lives. Like any playing field, this field must be maintained. Just because it looks good one season does not guarantee that it will be in perfect condition the next season. Coaching young athletes is a constant process; your work is never done. Once you have successfully laid the field your work is not over; in some sense it is just beginning. Some coaches will not have the opportunity to coach the same players the following year. If this is the case you start the same process over again with a new group of athletes. However, if you do get the opportunity to coach the same players for more than one season it is important to still go through the first four steps of the Ethical Youth Coaching Five Stages of Player

Development. However, with the insight gained from the previous season you will be able to go through the stages more confidently.

Stage: X

Going through the above steps deliberately and in order is, of course, not always realistic. Many coaches have only several months with their players and must prepare them for games by showing them the necessary skills. This being said, it is imperative that you don't abandon the above steps in favor of just teaching your players the nuts and bolts of the game. In order to handle this situation we suggest adopting the concept of the **temporary field.** When the Chicago Bears were building their new stadium they did not stop playing football; they played on a temporary field. A coach who focuses solely on developing players' character may lose sight of developing the athletic abilities of their players, and vice versa.

The concept of a temporary field is used primarily in the beginning stages, when a coach is most likely to get overwhelmed. As you build the stadium that will develop your players into well-rounded individuals who are able to discern life skills from their participation in sports, you can use the concept of the temporary field as a way to also focus on sports skills. Each individual coach will have to find his or her balance, but it is important to remember that like the Chicago Bears, a team must play while its permanent stadium is being built. As long as you blend the five stages of player development into your sports-specific coaching, you will excel. Let's look at two examples, one of a coach who perfectly balances building the stadium and temporary field, and one of a coach who does not balance the two correctly.

Coach A:

Coach A holds a pizza party at the beginning of the year in which he or she gets his or her players and parents together to outline the upcoming season. Coach A talks about the importance of showing up on time and gives the players a handout on sportsmanship. He also gives the players a handout on sports-specific drills they will be doing at practice. Coach A tells his players that the season is a progression of events and that they must develop both individually and as a team. In closing Coach A tells the players how excited he is for the start of the season and thanks the parents for their support, pointing out how important parental involvement is for their child's success.

Coach B:

Coach B holds his practice on the first day practices are allowed. Right from the start he has players engaging in intense sports-specific drills. During the second practice he divides up the team and has them play against each other, saying that the starters will come from the winning team. Right before the first game Coach B holds a brief meeting about sportsmanship and for the first time tells the team he is proud of them.

Hopefully you recognized that Coach A embodies the ethical youth coach and Coach B does not. Coach A lays the foundation at the first team meeting. Not only does he talk about sports-specific skills, but also addresses sportsmanship and the importance of teamwork. Furthermore, he brings the parents into the fold by inviting them to the meeting and addressing their importance (Chapter 14 discusses parental involvement in more detail). His example shows how you can balance the demands of getting players ready for their given sport with the concern for developing the complete player. Giving players information on sports-specific drills as well as on sportsmanship is a great strategy for achieving this balance.

In contrast, Coach B does not embody the principles of an EYC coach. Right from the beginning Coach B shows that his focus is on making his players competitive. There is nothing wrong with holding inner team games; just make sure that the focus is on developing game-time skills and team communication. Furthermore, the first time Coach B tells his team he is proud of them is right before the first game. If a coach is following the positive coaching model, he or she frequently tells players that he or she is proud of them. Coach B's motivation for expressing his pride may be little more than getting the team pumped up before the game.

One reason we separate the process of player development into five stages is that we want to emphasize its gradual nature. This is particularly important when dealing with young people whose attention spans are not always the longest, particularly when it comes to something as potentially boring as ethics. All kidding aside, a well-intentioned coach might be so eager after reading this book that he or she will want to talk about all the key components of ethical player development at the first meeting with his or her team. What this coach may not realize is that while his or her intentions are noble, he or she may actually be doing more harm than good. If this coach does not then immediately engage his or her players there is a possibility that they would thereafter completely tune him or her out the next time the concept of ethical player development is addressed. This is why we advocate a gradual approach. Little by little you will get your players to embrace the concepts set forth in this book. Before you know it you will be laying the field and providing them with skills that will last a lifetime.

The following five chapters break down each stage of player development and talk specifically about how you can implement them into your coaching practice. These chapters will highlight how each stage contributes to the four key characteristics of the ethical player and will offer insights into effective coaching techniques.

Keywords:

Laying the Foundation
Building the Frame
Exterior Finishes
Working on the Interior
Laying the Field
Positive Inner Speech
Temporary Field

Questions:

1) (True or False) Twenty percent of high school football players make it to the NFL.
2) (True or False) Simply participating in sports will ensure character development in young athletes.
3) How can you show more concern for character development in your players?
4) List the EYC Five Stages of Player Development.

5) Describe how positive inner speech is important when things are not going well on your team.
6) Explain how the concept of **the temporary field** is important to a coach.
7) Why is it important that you balance your desire to coach sports-specific tactics with ethical player development?

Activities:

1) Create an outline of your upcoming season utilizing the Five Stages of Player Development.

Chapter 5
Stage One:
Laying the Foundation
(Before First Practice)

What is a coach? Simply put, a coach is someone who guides a team. A coach designs practices, creates game plans and ensures that players receive proper instruction. Moreover, a coach is someone who sets the tone for the team. **Setting the tone** is particularly important for youth coaches. Children are quite observant, and how you present yourself as a coach can have a huge impact on the direction of the team. For example, a coach who shows up late and is dressed haphazardly will convey to his or her team that a casual approach is okay and discipline is of no importance. Conversely, a coach who is always early and dressed neatly will convey a polished image and as a result set a positive tone for the team.

The importance of how you present yourself to your young players cannot be overemphasized. Think back to when you were a young athlete – did the ways your coaches acted influence your behavior? Research indicates that children model the behavior of the adults in their environment, particularly parents and authority figures. As a coach, you are front and center, and viewed as an authority figure. What you do and say is being soaked up like a sponge. When you are frustrated and upset, so are your players. Always make sure you are utilizing the positive coaching model!

A coach must always have respect for the sport he or she coaches. This respect is encompassed by many variables; the following are not meant to be exhaustive. For instance, you should, of course, know the rules of the sport you are coaching. One great way to set a positive tone for your team is to present the rules of the sport either verbally or with handouts. Show your team that you are a student of the game. For example, while you are waiting for players to arrive have a coaching book by your side. This is a great way to show your team that you care; even young children will pick up on these small details. It is important to know the traditions of the sport you are coaching and share these traditions with your players.

Creating a learning environment goes hand in hand with respecting the sport you are coaching. In addition to providing players with information about the sport they are playing, always make sure you set aside time for players' questions. If you are using them, players' logs and binders are a great way to create a learning environment. Remember, any activity you implement should be fun. By creating a learning environment you are promoting education. This can go a long way in developing young athletes into better students. Studies have shown that participation in sports can improve children's performance in formal education (COE, D. P., J. M. PIVARNIK, 2006). As a coach you have a tremendous opportunity to enhance the educational experiences of your young athletes and help change society.

The **Coach as a Teacher Model** recognizes the importance that sport coaches have in imparting knowledge and setting a positive example for young athletes. In this model the playing field is seen as an extension of the classroom and the sport coach is seen as a kind of teacher. Not only are you imparting sports-based knowledge to young athletes, but you are also imparting motor skills that will benefit them for the rest of their lives.

A very important step you can take at the beginning of the season is to hold a team meeting and involve the parents in this meeting. If funds permit, having a pizza party during the meeting is a great way to get everyone in the spirit. Please do not serve alcohol to the parents at this meeting, as it is about the kids not about the parents getting together and "having a few." The pre-season team meeting is the main component of the first stage of player development. Below is a possible agenda for this initial meeting. Please note, this is only meant to be a guide; you can make adjustments based on your needs.

Party Plan:
- I) Introductions
- II) Distribute Team Rules
- III) Describe practice schedule and game schedule (distribute practice and game calendar). Describe what will take place during the season; perhaps show a sample practice plan.
- IV) Talk about your coaching philosophy (possibly distribute handouts that illustrate your coaching philosophy) and talk about player log binder.
- V) Hydration and nutrition presentation
- VI) Pass out "Special Circumstance" form (To be discussed shortly)
- VII) Closing notes before pizza. Ask both players and parents to go up to and meet two players/ parents they don't know during pizza)
- VIII) Pizza

Try to keep your speaking brief, as young people's attention spans are short and at this point your players are excited to get out and play. Furthermore, wait to unveil the pizza until after you have spoken on the main points, as the pizza will be a distraction when it is served. If a pizza party is not possible you can hold a meeting before the first practice and ask the parents to attend. Remember, the first team meeting is an important step in laying the foundation for your team's success. It is by laying this foundation that you will be able to instill the four key principles of the ethical player: Developmental Skills, Healthy Lifestyle, Sportsmanship and Team Building. Make sure that at least one parent or guardian of each child is present during the meeting. If a parent or guardian is not able to attend, send the team rules home with the child and have their parent(s) sign the rules as proof that they read them. It is okay to make parent attendance mandatory. You will be surprised at the compliance, because kids want to play.

It is important to be mindful of not going overboard during this initial meeting in describing your coaching philosophy and ethical principles. It is often easy to do this because there is no physical practice being conducted during the meeting and as a result a coach might think this is his or her big opportunity to give a dissertation on coaching. Don't forget that young people's attention spans can be limited. By inundating them with tons of coaching philosophy you lose their interest, and they will not be attentive to the most important aspects of this first presentation, i.e. team rules. This is where in stage one the concept of the temporary field comes into play. Your players are eager to get out on the field and start playing, not to listen to a coach talk endlessly about sportsmanship and team building. While you know that as an Ethical Youth Coach you have a responsibility to lay the foundation and teach players about these important topics, you must temper this with the understanding that if you push the concepts too hard too soon you may completely turn players off and as a result be unable to instill them. Therefore, as indicated above in the brief sample outline of your team meeting, when you hand out something that describes coaching philosophy (i.e. an article on sportsmanship), follow that up with handing out something sports-specific (i.e. a primer on baseball batting drills). This creates a nice balance that will keep the attention of your players and provide the foundation necessary to develop the complete player.

After you have introduced yourself the next thing you should do is distribute the team rules. The league for which you coach will undoubtedly have rules already in place; the suggestions below are meant to complement the leagues rules. During the meeting go over each rule and have everyone, including players, sign one copy to give to you and keep one copy for his or her reference. As stated earlier, if a player's parent(s) are unable to be present during this meeting make sure they sign and return one copy of the rules (you will thus be distributing two copies to all players).

Eagles Team Rules

1-The goal of this season is to have fun, practice and play hard, be a team and become better athletes.

2-Practice is critical to success. Therefore, participation in practice is essential. Players who miss a practice without permission will

be excused from the team with no exception. If you must miss a practice, please have your parent/ guardian call the coach.

3-If you are going to miss a game please notify the coach as early as possible.

4-Arrive on time for all games and practices. If practice starts at 1:00 it is advised that you arrive at 12:45. Great players always arrive early.

5-Appropiate dress for practice is required. If a player is not dressed appropriately they will not practice. During the initial meeting players and parents will be made aware of appropriate attire.

6-You must wear the league uniform during all games and also league mandated safety gear. Anyone in violation will not play.

7-Up to a two week absence from the season for family vacation, special schooling, or family activities is allowed. The coach must be notified in writing two weeks in advance.

8-During all games and practices we stay together as a team. Players cannot meet with outside friends or coaches unless directed to do so by the coach.

9-A coach will notify you when a game or practice is cancelled.

10-No foul or obscene language will be tolerated in any form.

11-Players will show respect to all coaches (including the opposing coaches), parents, fans and league officials. Only a coach will dispute bad calls or issues with refs.

12-Players will respect and care for all team equipment.

13-We monitor grades! Any players receiving a grade lower than a C has one week to improve the grade to C or better. If the player is unable to bring the grade up they will not practice or play until the grade is brought up.

14-If a player has broken a school rule and received punishment from the school the player will also receive a team consequence determined by the coach. *This only applies to school teams.*

15-Academics are your number one priority. However, having homework or a test is not an excuse for missing a game or practice. Athletes must learn to use their time efficiently. If you are having difficulty with balancing the demands of school and sports see the coach for help.

Signed (Player): _____ Date: _____

Signed (Parent): _____ Date: _____

Signed (Coach): _____ Date: _____

After you have gone over the rules it is important that you go over the consequences of violating the rules. Because an EYC coach does not use running as a punishment, the primary means a coach has for enforcing the team rules is taking away playing time and ultimately, if the violations are serious enough, removing the player from the team. Below is a sample plan for rule violations. This plan is for your personal use and should not be distributed; you will verbally inform your team of the consequences of rule violations. The most important thing for enforcing rules is consistency. It is up to the individual coach to use his or her judgment in determining the seriousness of the violation.

Minor Violation:
Verbal recognition of violation and indication that a second violation will result in a major violation. Common offenses: uniform violation, slightly late to practice, swearing (up to coach to determine if swear word and use is minor).

Major Violation:
Sit out practice and/or game. Common offenses: excessive swearing, bullying, lack of respect for coach or fellow players, excessively late, excessive uniform violations, vacation policy violation, academic violation.

Serious Violation:
Sit out several games and potential removal from team. Common offenses: violence, abusive behavior towards fellow players, repeated major violations.

Presenting the team rules and verbally discussing how you will handle violations of these rules is a critical element to the first team meeting. Make sure you are prepared to make this presentation and seek to be as concise as possible. If your league has a rulebook, distribute it to the players and parents. However, we recommend that you only go over the most relevant rules from the book, as they tend to be quite long.

While looking at the outline you probably wondered what the "Hydration Presentation" entails. One of the most neglected areas of youth sports is hydration. Coaches are so busy coaching that they forget to monitor their players' hydration. This can have disastrous consequences. By making your players and parents aware of the importance of hydration you make your job a little easier during the season. There is no need to go into a long-winded presentation on the science behind hydration. The following is a list of what you should present.

Hydration
-60% of the body is composed of water.

-Pediatricians recommend that children drink half their body weight in ounces of water per day (i.e. an eighty pound child should drink forty ounces of water per day).

-It is critical to hydrate well before games and practices. In general, starting two hours before practices or games a player should consume 12-16 ounces of water.

-When it is hot and for practices lasting over ninety minutes the use of electrolyte drinks may be warranted (i.e. Gatorade).

-Throughout practices and games continue to sip water.

-It is important to hydrate after practices and games. The first twenty minutes after a game or practice are critical for maintaining hydration. Parents should have cold, fresh water available for their children.

You should also have players and parents fill out a **Special Circumstance Form** (bullet point six on meeting outline). This is an important way to gain insight into any special issues that may arise with players, particularly any medical conditions (i.e. heart conditions). In many leagues this important information is not shared with coaches in a timely manner, so even if the league does this, have your own. Have players or their parents fill out a little note card with their names and at the end of the meeting hand the cards back to you. It is important to keep this information confidential and be discreet when handling these forms after they are handed in at the end of the meeting. You never know parents' comfort level with other people knowing the information they have provided about their child.

Holding a team meeting is a great way to get to know your team and is critical to the first stage of player development. Don't be intimidated by all the suggestions in this chapter. With a little planning and work you will be a pro in no time.

Action Steps:
-Set up a team meeting prior to the first practice
-Create an outline of what you are going to say at the team meeting
-Print any handouts that will be distributed at the meeting
-Have fun!

Keywords:
Setting the Tone

Coach as a Teacher Model
Team Rules
Special Circumstance Form

Questions:

1) Why is how you present yourself to your team important?
2) Name two ways in which a coach can set the tone for his or her team.
3) How can a coach show respect for the sport he or she is coaching?
4) (True or False) Sports can enhance a child's academic performance.
5) How can a coach create a learning environment?
6) (True or False) You should eat right at the start of your team's preseason meeting.
7) (True or False) You should speak a lot during the preseason team meeting.
8) Name the three levels of rule violations.
9) What percentage of the body is composed of water?

Suggested Activities:

1) Print out a brief history of the sport you are coaching and distribute it to your players.
2) Create your preseason meeting agenda.
3) Pizza at the preseason meeting notwithstanding, at team meetings hand out healthy snacks and discuss how these snacks can help players become better athletes by providing the proper nutrition for their bodies.

Chapter 6
Stage Two:
Building the Frame (Practices 1-5)

Now that you have laid the foundation at your team meeting it is time to turn our attention to the first few practices. Stage two occurs at the start of the very first practice and lasts up until the fifth practice. Please note, this timeline is merely a suggestion and is not a rule set in stone. Some coaches may find that two practices are sufficient for this stage while others may hold seven. The length of your season may also have a bearing on how long you have to develop the team in this stage. For coaches working with very little time before games start (very common for summer leagues), two practices may be all the time you have. If you find yourself in this situation, don't panic – just make sure you come to the first practice ready to go. The primary focus during this stage is on team building as a whole; the reasoning behind this will soon become clear. Let's first discuss some skills that a coach should posses in order to implement this stage successfully.

One area that you should be prepared for at the start of the first practice is **assessing players**. Some experienced coaches will find assessing players a piece of cake, particularly those who are familiar with many of the players on the team. However, for the inexperienced coach assessing players need not be difficult. In order to assess players you simply need an open mind and a little preparation. It is important to draw as little attention as possible to your player assessment and for the purposes of the EYC program this assessment is not meant for coaching situations where you must "cut players." This assessment strategy is meant to give you a framework for better understanding your team as a whole and successfully utilizing the EYC winning factor, a valuable technique that will be introduced later. Because this assessment is internal it is best to write your notes after practice, when your team has left. The reasoning behind this is that you don't want your players to think you are "sizing them up" (which creates tension for them). This would be hard to avoid if during the first few practices you are writing on a clip board. Throughout the season you will be constantly gaining insight on your players, but for the purposes of this assessment allow yourself 2-3 practices. You will want to have a roster of your players available at the end of practice so that you can assess them. The following are the five basic areas you will be assessing your players on.

Assessment   **Rating 1-5** (1=Low Ability, 5=High Ability)
Athletic Ability
Motor Skills
Coordination
Understanding of game
Enthusiasm for game

With the cumulative scores from this rating system you will likely get the following **Four Talent Levels**:

High Talent (HT) 20> (Typically 10% fall into this group)

Above Average Talent (AAT) 15> (Typically 20% fall into this group)

Average Talent (AT) 10> (Typically 60% fall into this group)

Below Average Talent (BAT) 9< (Typically 10% fall into this group)

As an EYC coach you must understand that this data is simply a snapshot of your team and not a set-in-stone evaluation. This information is meant to be a starting point that will help you set your lineup for your first few games. Don't be afraid to change your assessment as the season progresses. Keep in mind that this is not a "**scout evaluation**" and is not meant to be comprehensive. It is important not to agonize over this. Use your instincts! For coaches with assistants divide up the assessments. You should be spending no more than five minutes per player on the written portion of the assessment. One of the wonderful benefits of doing this assessment is how much it makes you comfortable with your role as a coach. Ask any teacher – this same kind of exercise in the first few days of class each year is an important survival skill. If a teacher doesn't quickly size up what these students are going to be like, the school year can get off to a terrible start.

Now let's focus our discussion on how this stage addresses the four areas of ethical youth player development.

Developmental Skills

Helping your team and players set goals will be one of the greatest areas of impact on their developmental skills during stage two. Setting goals should begin during the second practice and continue throughout the rest of the season. Goal-setting is unique to each team and coach. Your team's goals should come in three different forms: daily, weekly and season-long. Below is an example of a team's goals.

Tigers Basketball Team Goals
-*Daily: Make sixty percent of free throws in practice.*
-*Weekly: Win game against Lions.*
-*Season: Win eighteen games and win the championship.*

You will need to help players eleven and under verbally establish their personal goals. Their goals will be verbal because this age range of players will not be keeping written logs. Remember, younger players have a more "self-centered" and immediate focus and while it is important to establish team goals like the ones above, they are not going to have the same motivational impact as they will for older players. Telling an eight year old that it is important to practice free throws for one hour because it will help them win the championship two months down the line is not going to have the immediate impact that coaches want. Focusing on the present is much more effective, while occasionally reminding them of long-term goals. If a young player's goal is to make more free throws, focus on the success of making each free throw and not so much on "pumping" up the player on how his or her free throw ability will help the team win the championship.

For players twelve and older you will write team goals directly on their practice and game plans, and have them write in their own personal goals. Goal-setting is a great way for players to understand the importance of establishing a goal and then working towards that goal step by step. Effectively helping your team towards a goal is one of the greatest developmental skills a coach can impart to their players. Always be positive with your players, even when there are setbacks. It is your responsibility to help your team establish realistic goals. If your team won only two games in the previous season and the same team is back again, it may be unrealistic to set a goal of going undefeated. Perhaps in this case you can set a goal of winning half of your games. However, you must temper your realism with a sense of optimism. Encourage your team and players to set challenging goals, ones that will help them achieve things they never thought possible. One of the greatest gifts sports gives us is the ability to witness people achieve things that they never thought were possible.

Coaches by nature are observant. From the very first formal practice you will notice various things about your players. One such thing you should be on the look out for right from the beginning is how confidently each player approaches practice. Detecting a player's confidence level is both an art and a skill. As a coach you will get better at detecting confidence as you progress in your coaching. The key is to be mindful of the **confidence levels** of your players. One way you can evaluate player confidence levels is gauging their eagerness to volunteer. Observe which players immediately raise their hand or jump at the opportunity to volunteer. Look for the players who are reluctant, and when you have selected the volunteer observe if any of the players looked relieved. Another method to assess confidence is to observe if they are fearful of the sport. Do they shirk away from the ball? Do they avoid physical contact? When you have identified the players whose confidence levels are low it is time to devise some strategies to boost these confidence levels. Here is a list of some things to look for when identifying players with low confidence levels.

-Eagerness to volunteer. Does the player shy away from volunteer opportunities?

-Willingness to sit out during a game. Does the player appear content not to play?

-Body Language when playing. How does the young athlete carry himself or herself? Do they stand tall? Do they look down at the ground or at their opponent?

-Level of fear.

Now that you have identified the players with lower levels of confidence it is time to boost their confidence. This does not mean that you immediately start to put players on the spot and call on them every time you need a volunteer. It is best to start out more generally. Because you are already committed to the Ethical Youth Coaching model you are coaching in a style that allows your players to be comfortable around you. However, evaluate your adherence to the principles set forth by the Center for Ethical Youth Coaching. If you determine that you are lacking in a few areas make adjustments to get back on the right path. We call the above **assessing your coaching**. During stage two of player development the two best ways of addressing players' confidence levels is to first make a general address about the importance of confidence in sports. Second, expose the fearful player to the actions of the game. Fear typically comes from the unknown. The more you make things familiar, the more confidence the player will develop. The general address is best accomplished during a team meeting. Come prepared with an example of a famous player from the sport you are coaching and how this athlete embodies the confident athlete. Use the meeting to point out how failure is okay and it is a natural part of sports. Again, having a few examples of famous athletes at hand would be great (i.e. Michael Jordan was cut from his high school basketball team). Under no circumstances should you point out specific players during this meeting and this means even pointing out examples of confident players on the team. If you highlight a player who currently is displaying low levels of confidence you are embarrassing the player and potentially hurting the player's self-esteem. Remember, as coaches we have a duty to do nothing that damages players' self-esteem.

Healthy Lifestyle

As a sports coach you are in a wonderful position to teach children about the importance of a healthy lifestyle. The fact that these young people are participating in a physical activity and not sitting in front of the television playing video games is a great start. A coach with dubious ethical standards can turn away a young person from sports and physical activity. It is important to promote not only athletic performance to your young athletes but also a healthy lifestyle. Early in the season it is important to keep the practices light and focus on gradually building intensity. Many coaches, in an effort to maximize time, ramp up the intensity of practices too fast, which causes players to become fatigued and burned out. The reason why this approach to practice is so popular is that it gets immediate results. By putting extreme amounts of stress on the body the body is forced to adapt. Because young bodies are resilient they are able to recover quickly and handle the stress for short periods of time. The fact that most sports seasons are relatively short allows the overloaded intensity to go undetected. According to studies by the Institute for the Study of Youth Sports, drop out rates are as high as 50% by the time young athletes reach early adolescence. One of the reasons for this high number is the burn out that happens as a result of too much too soon. Players simply become tired from putting their body through the stress of rapidly increasing their training. As a result, when many of these young athletes are done playing, they want nothing to do with activity in general and lead a sedentary lifestyle. The very thing sports is supposed to promote, an active lifestyle, it in fact turns people away from.

In addition to the over-training that occurs in many youth sports circles, several other unhealthy practices are not recommended. Another big offense seen in youth sports is unhealthy eating and weight management practices. Two prominent American sports that are repeat offenders are football and wrestling. How many reading this book have encountered the high school linemen coach who advocates methods such as eating a huge meal right before bed (in addition to three regular meals throughout the day) in order to "bulk up" for the season? How many have encountered the wrestling coach who advocates saunas as a way to drop "water weight"? Not only are these practices grossly unhealthy, but they also give young athletes the wrong message about how to treat their bodies. An athlete should be in tune with his or her body and treat it with the utmost respect. Another common offense is the early morning practice. These types of practices typically occur at the high school level as a way to get in extra practice. Typically they're disguised as "early morning conditioning" and are "voluntary" (note, they are only voluntary if you do not want to play on the team). Many of these early morning sessions begin at 6am, meaning that some young athletes have to wake up as early as 4:30am. So even if a player goes to bed at 10pm they would only get six and a half hours of sleep. This is two and a half hours less than is medically recommended. With all the academic demands placed on high school students this loss of sleep can be devastating. As an Ethical Youth Coach it is up to you to put an end to these practices. This means not only not engaging in these practices yourself, but also attempting to educate other coaches on the dangers. Of course, some coaches may argue that their players like to win and if they do not engage in these practices there are other coaches who are willing to do these things so that their teams will have a competitive edge. No one said that being an Ethical Youth Coach was going to be a cakewalk. The EYC motto is, **"Winning is something, but not everything."** Furthermore, a rested player who has gradually built up his or her conditioning will be in far better shape to perform at the end of the season!

Sportsmanship

During stage two of player development you will not be playing against other teams and therefore not be able to directly observe the sportsmanship displayed by your players towards other teams. However, you will be able to observe one dimension of sportsmanship by how your players interact with each other. Just because there are no games does not mean you cannot work on sportsmanship. At the end of practice, during your team meeting, make a point to talk about honoring your opponent and the importance of never taunting them. By addressing these issues at this stage you will be planting a seed for the games later on.

Team Building

One of the reasons why you focus on the whole team during this stage is your concern for developing team unity. When you begin to work with individual players there is a possibility that some players may view this as favoritism (even though this is not the case). By keeping your focus on the whole team for the first few practices you are establishing to everyone the importance of the team. This will make it easier when you begin to place more focus on individual players. Therefore, a simple, effective way to work on team building during stage two is to make sure you keep your focus on the team. This is not to say that you turn a blind eye when a player comes up to you with an individual question. What we are advocating is that during these first few practices your emphasis should be on the team as a whole. Let's take a look at an example to illustrate the correct and the incorrect way to handle team building during this stage.

Coach A:

Coach A coaches boys' soccer and is conducting his second practice of the year. He coaches sixteen boys all under 10 and he is the only coach. During this practice he works with each player individually on ball handling and takes very little time to address the team as a whole. While working with individual players he spends a disproportionate amount of time with certain players that need special attention. Coach A conducts the whole practice in this manner and then concludes the practice by individually critiquing the players in front of the whole team.

Coach B:

Coach B also coaches a boys' soccer team and is conducting his second practice of the year. He coaches sixteen boys all under 10 and he is the only coach. During this practice he has players pair up and work on ball handling drills. Every ten minutes he has players switch partners. He conducts the whole practice in this manner and while observing the players he goes up to players that are having difficulty and offers guidance. He also involves the partner in this instruction. At the end of the practice he addresses the whole team, pointing out the positives of the team's ball handling skills. He also addresses the areas that players need to work on.

Hopefully you identified that Coach B more closely adheres to the Ethical Youth Coaching Model. While Coach A appears to be a caring coach who wants to see the players succeed by focusing his sole attention on individual players, he is doing little to foster team unity. It is inevitable that Coach A will spend more time with certain players and as a result have less time to spend with other players. This will lead the other players to feel neglected, and spiteful of their fellow teammates. Furthermore, at the end of practice Coach A specifically points out the positives and negatives of each player's performance. While this will boost the confidence of the players that performed well it will damage the confidence of the players who need improvement. Even if Coach A is careful in his criticism he will still be creating a divide. This early in the season the team may not have the unity to absorb the divide created by individual critiques.

On the other hand Coach B perfectly implements the principles of the Ethical Youth Coaching Model. Coach B's team is only on their second practice; they have yet to "gel" as a team. Coach B pairs them up to work on drills and then, to ensure that they have exposure to different teammates, he switches their partners. While they are engaging in these drills he walks around and addresses individual needs, but he also makes sure to involve the partner. By doing this he is creating a team bond without putting the player on the spot. Being singled out can be incredibly embarrassing for the player this early in the season, when players can still be unsure of their skills. At the end of the practice Coach B talks to the whole team about the specific things he observed during the practice. However, he does not put anyone on the spot by pointing out particular players.

For the skeptical coach reading this right now and wondering how their team can get better if he or she is not able to spend significant amounts of time with players that need more help, your answer comes in the next chapter, which focuses more on individual players. Remember, the five stages of player development is a gradual process, and you cannot start working on the interior of the stadium if the frame is not yet built. If you are coaching in a situation where you have an assistant coach, your strategy during this stage does not change. Consider yourself lucky that you have another set of eyes!

Remember, your focus during this stage of player development is on building team unity. Your attention should be directed toward the team as a whole. The next stage will allow you to focus more on individual skill building.

Keywords:
Building the frame
Assessing your coaching
Assessing your players
Four Talent Levels
Scout Evaluation

Questions:
1) (True or False) The length of the season can determine how long you have to develop Stage Two.
2) Why is it important that a coach directs his or her attention toward the team as a whole during this stage?
3) Describe how an EYC coach assesses players.
4) (True or False) An EYC coach evaluation is the same as a "scout evaluation."
5) Why is it important to assess your coaching?
6) What are the four talent levels used for the EYC player assessment?
7) List and describe the importance of the three different types of goals.
8) List two areas you should evaluate when you determine player confidence levels.
9) Is working on sportsmanship important during this stage and if so, why?

10) (True or False) Youth sports have drop out rates as high as 70%.

Suggested Activities:

1) Create your own player assessment template, using the one provided in this chapter as a model.

Chapter 7
Stage Three: Exterior Finishes

Now that you have laid the foundation and built the frame, it is time to put on the final touches before your first game. Many coaches reading this manual have probably been wondering when they would be able to ramp up their practices and start intensively addressing individual player skills. Stage three, which we call **exterior finishes**, is when we advocate ramping up the intensity of practices and addressing individual players. Now, this does not mean you abandon your focus on the team as a whole. Like the process of building a stadium, **constant vigilance** must be maintained with the whole structure in order for it to be sound. Remember, this book is not focused on the sports-specific side of training. However, the Ethical Youth Coach is responsible for having a proper understanding of how to implement and measure skill development. Appendix C contains a list of resources that point you in the right direction for the sports-specific side of training.

Stage three will take us all the way up to the first game of your season. As a coach who follows the Ethical Youth Coaching Model there are several things you will want to be aware of during this stage. Your team now has several practices under their belt and some fatigue may begin to set in. The saying, "no pain, no gain" has no credence with the Ethical Youth Coach. Make sure you inform your players that rest is very important for athletes and is indeed a key to success. High school coaches, make sure you tell your athletes that burning the midnight oil is ill advised for optimal athletic performance.

By now you have a clearer idea of who your "star" players are and it is important that these players receive equal treatment. Conversely you have identified the players on your team who need extra attention.

While it is crucial that you develop these players and work with them to develop their talents it is also imperative that you do not create a situation in which your sole attention is focused on a handful of players. This is not an effective strategy primarily for two reasons: 1) other players are not getting the attention they need; no matter how good a player is there is always something they could be working on, and 2) you could potentially be creating a division on the team by focusing on a few select players. As a coach you never want to hear "Why is she so special?" A great coach is like a master tight-rope walker, always balancing the various demands of his or her team. Like a tight-rope walker, if you focus too much on one side you fall! One way to offer additional help to players is by letting players know that you will be arriving to practice early, and any players who want to work on specific areas are welcome to come. Another possible strategy to assist players that need additional help is to recommend to the whole team outside training centers where they can receive one-on-one instruction. The key to this recommendation is that you are addressing the whole team and not going up to individual players and telling them to "get outside help." Make sure you trust the places you recommend and have checked them out. Now let's begin our discussion of the four key areas of player development.

Developmental Skills

Now that you have entered into stage three you have had a chance to observe your team during at least two practices, but hopefully five or more practices. During these practices you have probably gained an understanding of the developmental levels of your players. You have identified which players readily volunteer for drills and which players shy away. You have identified which players are eager to try something again after they have not succeeded and which players quickly move on to something different. For the most part, up until now, you have allowed the players to show you their developmental levels and have done little to intervene. You have talked to the team about the importance of confidence, goal setting, focus and determination. Your actions have been directed towards building these skills, but they have not yet been tailored to maximize each individual player's developmental skills. As a coach it is always important to remember to frame everything in the positive. This is particularly important during stage three, as the practices are ramping up and you will undoubtedly be engaging your players in numerous drills, thus increasing the probability of players making mistakes. Let's take a look at a hypothetical situation and two possible ways of handling it.

Coach A

Coach A is teaching her players how to catch a softball that is hit over their head. One player keeps trying to back-pedal rather than turning and running back for the ball. After repeated attempts in which the coach yells, "you screwed it up, let's try again," the coach gives up and tells the player she better work on this at home.

Coach B

Coach B is teaching her players how to catch a softball that is hit over their head. One player keeps trying to back-pedal rather then turning and running back for the ball. After the first unsuccessful attempt, Coach B makes sure the player understands the motions of the drill. Once the player has demonstrated an understanding of the mechanics of the drill the coach attempts the drill again. The player is again unsuccessful. This time the coach is quick to point out that the player looked better this time and indicates they are going to try it one more time, but that she should try to be more relaxed this time. The player again is not successful and as a result the coach tells the player that they will work more on this later and, not to worry, she will be a master in no time.

You may have noticed that the description of Coach B's handling of the situation is much longer than Coach A's. This helps draw out another principle of the Center for Ethical Youth Coaching, "**Good Coaching Takes Time.**" An impatient coach will struggle with the Ethical Youth Coaching Model because their desire to rush to the finish will cause them to gloss over important areas of player development. Coach B's approach exemplifies the Ethical Youth Coach. Coach B takes a patient approach and attempts to show the player how to succeed. When the player is unable to complete the drill

Coach B reassures the player that she will be successful and promises to work with the player more later. Coach B does not lose her cool and does not put the player on the spot. She thus creates an environment in which her players feel relaxed and are able to focus on what is important, playing sports. It is also important to note that Coach B does not continue with the drill and offer no guidance. Furthermore, sometimes a player needs to be removed from the drill for a while in order for the player to process the motions of the drill and for them to have a chance to visualize success. It is vitally important that you reinforce that they will be successful next time they attempt the drill. Coaches like Coach A feel they are doing the player justice by continually repeating the drill, with no guidance, until they are successful. Oftentimes these coaches create a frustrating situation in which they begin to say derogatory things while the player is attempting the drill. Most coaches will hang their hat on the principle that repetition is the key to success. While this sentiment is true, the type of repetition that is occurring for Coach A's player is not effective because it is being reinforced through **negative coaching**. In essence, coaches like Coach A are attempting to intimidate their players into succeeding and not allowing them to develop the confidence necessary to complete the drill of their own accord. You do not have to look far to see the ramifications this coaching style has for other areas of an individual's life. Coach A is creating an environment in which people are motivated by the will of those above them, whereas Coach B is creating an environment in which she motivates people to succeed of their own accord. It is important to recognize the difference between **Motivating versus Imposing Your Will**. Motivating is giving positive affirmations to your players in the hope that they will succeed. Imposing your will is demanding that players adhere to your standards and relentlessly pursue the activity until you are satisfied. Confidence cannot be willed into players; it must be nurtured and developed over time. As an EYC coach you must focus on building your players' internal motivation.

Healthy Lifestyle

Stage three of player development presents the coach with a great opportunity to show players how to cope with increased stress on the body. At this point your practices are ramping up and the aerobic stress is increasing. As a result, rest and recovery is crucial to the success of your players. Now, coaches who coach young children might be quick to dismiss this section. However, just because your players' youth allows them to bounce back quickly does not mean you cannot educate them on the importance of rest and recovery. It is still important that all age groups understand the importance of healthy eating and how carbohydrates and protein aid in their recovery. The only thing that changes across age groups is the level at which you present the information. The mentality of "they are young and they can worry about that later" is not part of the Ethical Youth Coach's vocabulary. Teaching your players how to lead a healthy lifestyle may be the greatest gift that you can give them as a coach. According to the Centers for Disease Control and Prevention, one-third of Americans are obese, and this number keeps increasing. This number is shocking, and should be unacceptable to anyone who calls him- or herself a coach. As a coach you can play an integral role in helping curb the obesity epidemic. The following are some specific strategies for helping players adopt healthy habits.

It starts with you

This may be hard for some coaches to accept. However, you are in front of the children you coach and as was explained earlier in this book a child often models what they see. If you are exhibiting unhealthy practices your players are absorbing this, and your behaviors may validate their unhealthy choices. Therefore, it is very important that your actions promote a healthy lifestyle.

Healthy Snacks

While there is nothing wrong with a little indulgence such as the time-honored tradition of ice cream after the game, there should also be emphasis placed on healthy snacks. Carrots and apples make a nice choice instead of always rotating between brownies and cupcakes. While undoubtedly you will have players who dismiss these healthy snacks, be quick to point out the benefits of these foods to their athletic performance.

Team Meetings

During one of your team meetings make it a point to dedicate some time to talking about the importance of leading a healthy lifestyle. The following are some sample topics to cover.

-Importance of sleep

-Having a balanced diet

-Drinking enough water (remember, we stressed that you talk about this at the pre-season meeting)

Sportsmanship

At this point games have still not begun; therefore, you have not had a chance to observe the sportsmanship displayed by your team toward other teams. The same advice from the previous stage holds true: work in the concept of good sportsmanship during team meetings and talk about how honoring your opponent makes your victories even greater. Oftentimes coaches will talk down about opponents in order to motivate their team. This is not an acceptable practice. For example, a coach who tells his team they are the hardest working team in the league is doing nothing wrong. It is when the coach tells his or her team that all the other teams are lazy that they are crossing the line. We will talk about this topic more in the next chapter. However, for now it suffices to say that calling the other teams in your league "chumps" is not acceptable.

Team Building

Stage three is a great time to really start addressing the chemistry on your team. By now you have gotten several practices under your belt and have had ample opportunity to observe how the players on your team interact with each other. Furthermore, as the intensity of the practices begins to heat up you have a chance to observe how your team interacts under pressure and stress. In the previous stages the importance of addressing the whole team was stressed and the coach was told to be cautious of focusing too much attention on individual players. This was done in order to create an environment in which the player was assured of the importance of the team and also to guarantee that everyone received equal treatment. During this stage you turned some of your focus to individual players. Now you have the chance to observe how this "extra" attention changes the team dynamic. Your players have also had a chance to formulate their opinions about their fellow teammates.

During this stage it is extremely important to be mindful of how your players treat each other. If you notice mild cases of certain players exerting their superiority over other players it may be best to broadly address the issue during a team meeting by talking about how everyone on the team is equal. However, if you notice extreme cases of players flaunting their talents to fellow teammates you must address the issue immediately and directly. Upon initial address of the issue make it known to the player who is acting superior that this type of activity is not to be tolerated. Make this first address brief and public. The reason for making this address public is to allow others on the team to know that this type of behavior will not be tolerated. Remember, we do not advocate yelling, and during this address your tone should be firm and even. In advocating that you make this address in public we are not recommending that you make a grandiose display. Coaches who are amateur directors, this is not your chance to create high drama. In the chapter on special situations we will be addressing the issue of bullying; coaches who are dealing with extreme cases will find their answers in that chapter.

To ensure that your players are learning how to work with each other it is important that you make sure they are continually interacting with different players on the team. In the first few practices (for new teams) this often happens naturally as players are socializing. However, as you enter stage three players have started to form **cliques** and oftentimes they will conduct warm ups and drills with the same group of individuals (i.e. baseball players playing catch with the same person every time). While these small, intimate groups often lead to strong friendships that endure outside of the sports realm it is still important to make sure your players are interacting with different people on the team. This does not mean it is wrong for your players to form close friendships, in fact this is one of the great benefits of sports – the lasting relationships created. As a coach it is your responsibility to get your team working as a unit. The most effective way to do this is by making sure your players are comfortable working with everyone on the team.

During stage three the most important thing to keep in mind is balance. Now that you have begun to place more emphasis on the individual player it is important to balance this with your need to develop the whole team. Remember, as was stated at the beginning of this chapter, a coach is a tight-rope walker whose goal is to keep everything in balance. At times keeping your balance can be difficult, but as long as you focus and take your time you will successfully reach the end of the tight-rope.

Action Steps:

-Temper your need to focus on individual players with your concern for the whole team.

-Discuss the importance of rest and healthy eating in athletic performance and recovery.

- Continue to make sure players interact with other players. Avoid cliques.

Key Words:

Exterior Finishes
Constant Vigilance
Good Coaching Takes Time
Negative Coaching
Motivating versus Imposing Your Will
Cliques

Study Questions:
1) Why is it important to maintain a constant vigilance with the whole team?
2) Why is rest important in sports?
3) Name two reasons why it is important not to focus your attention on a select few players.
4) A great coach is like a _____
5) What are the two strategies for assisting players who need additional help?

6) Why will an impatient coach struggle with the EYC model?

7) (True or False) It is always the prudent approach to continue a drill until a player masters the drill.

8) Describe how motivating is different from imposing your will.

9) According to the Centers for Disease Control and Prevention, what percentage of Americans are obese?

10) How does sportsmanship fit into stage three of player development?

11) (True or False) If a player is flaunting his or her talents incessantly to another player you should intervene.

12) Why is it important to avoid cliques?

Suggested Activities:

1) Come up with a list of creative ways to motivate your team. Start by searching the Internet for "great speeches" and go from there. Make sure you put all your ideas into your team folder.

Chapter 8
Stage Four: Working on the Interior

The moment everyone has been waiting for, Game Time! Stage four, also known as **working on the interior,** is when your team starts to play games. Working on the interior is a perfect metaphor for this stage because, like working on the interior of any structure, your work is never really complete. You are always making refinements and repairs to the interior. At the end of the day it is your belief in the foundation and exterior that allows you to feel confident in the soundness of the structure. As a coach it is your belief in the foundation you lay during pre-season practices that allows you to approach the season with confidence. Coaches who have teams with particularly demanding schedules will need to rely heavily on the foundation and exterior they build. While it may be easy to think that the EYC model only applies to the "practice season" and once the games start the "**win at all costs model**" comes back into play, this is not the case. This chapter will address how to implement the EYC model in the regular season.

The Importance of Winning

Some coaches may argue that their players want to win and the things they do are in the sprit of winning. A classic manifestation of this mentality is allowing only the best players to play. Depending on what level you coach this can be a tricky issue. In the view of the Center for Ethical Youth Coaching, for those who coach children at the grade school level, this should not be much of an issue. At this level winning is a bonus! The most important aspect of coaching young children is to promote proper technique and develop the four areas of the ethical youth player (Developmental Skills, Healthy Lifestyle, Sportsmanship and Teamwork). The level at which playing time becomes a more difficult issue is in high school, particularly at the Varsity level. Still, your primary focus should be on developing proper technique and developing the four areas of the character development side. However, it would be naïve to advocate that a coach block out winning from their vocabulary and allow every player equal playing time regardless of their talent level.

Remember the CEYC slogan, "Winning is something, but not everything." Winning is something: it can mean a trophy at the end of the year or a trip "down state." Winning can be a tremendous source of pride for your players and boost their confidence to new heights. Winning also means losing, which can also be a good thing, as it teaches your players how to cope with setbacks. In life you will undoubtedly encounter numerous setbacks. Your ability to deal with them is essential to being a successful individual. An athlete who knows how to lose in as dignified a way as he or she wins has a powerful tool for the rest of their lives. Winning can also mean better scholarship opportunities for college.

With all these positive aspects of winning, the question becomes, why does the CEYC advocate that coaches focus less on winning? Because winning also brings out the worst in teams. A coach whose sole focus is winning oftentimes abandons his or her ethical principles and adopts a "win at all costs" mentality. This mentality is often accompanied by extreme emotions from both the coach and players. These extremes of emotion often lead to inappropriate language and lack of sportsmanship. Young players should be focused on having fun, developing motor skills and character development. A coach that allows winning to dictate the direction of his or her team is doing a disservice to his or her players.

The correct way to handle the concept of winning in youth sports can be a complex issue and the opinions expressed by the coaching community vary. Some leagues choose to not keep score during games. Quite often these "**no score leagues**" are for children under the age of 10. While the intentions behind these leagues can be viewed as admirable, some of the reasoning offered by this model is quite polarizing and ultimately there are more effective ways to handle the concept of winning. There is no better way to get a coach in a heated debate than to discuss the relative merits of "everyone is a winner." An EYC coach understands that participation in youth sports has huge benefits to the player and that, win or lose, every player is drawing something positive from their participation. The winning and losing part of sports is one of the important aspects that helps develop the four key areas of player development. Amongst the areas most directly touched by winning is confidence. A win can do wonders for a player's confidence, and a loss, when handled incorrectly, can damage a player's confidence.

The Winning Factor

In order to handle the concept of winning and losing the CEYC has developed the notion of the **Winning Factor.** The winning factor is a gradual approach to introducing the importance of winning into the team dynamic. As was stated before, your emphasis as a coach is always to develop the complete player (sports-specific side and character development side). However, winning and losing are a component of sports and they must be addressed. For the most part, if you focus on developing the complete player, winning will take care of itself. However, the concepts brought up in discussing the winning factor will allow you to effectively deal with the intangibles that accompany winning and losing. Please note, the percent of focus is only meant to give you an idea of how to prioritize your emphasis on winning and how to handle the increased "perception" of winning (this will become clearer shortly). The **perception of winning** refers to the relative emphasis that different age groups place on the importance of winning. Of course, a win and a loss are the same no matter what age group you coach, but the importance a six year-old places on a win versus a sixteen year-old is markedly different. The perception of winning also encompasses individuals with an interest in the team. Expectations to win can be great for them, particularly parents who have invested a lot of time in their child's sporting career. Typically, like the players, those interested in the team place a greater level of importance on winning when players are older. As an EYC it is your job to adapt to this perception of winning and make sure it does not become a distraction in complete player development.

Winning Factor, 5-7 years old (10% focus)

At this stage your focus on winning should be 10% or less. Most of your players will not be as concerned about winning at this stage. Most likely their reactions to a win or loss will be shaped by their parents' reactions. It is important to make sure the parents are aware that at this level it is important that everyone plays and that you are working almost exclusively to promote their development. When your team wins focus on the hard work that led to this victory. When your team loses focus on what the team can work on to improve their play the next time. It is never acceptable to punish a team for a loss! It is important to not incessantly mention your team's record and "how many games they are out of first by." Furthermore, keeping individual stats is not advised at this level. Many little league baseball coaches think it is fun to give their players weekly stat sheets with batting averages. However, at this level it does nothing to promote their development as players. The only time you should talk specifically about stats is when educating your players about the game they are playing (i.e., what their favorite player's batting average means). If you are in a league where there is a championship at the end of the year it is important to tell your players how working together as a team and respecting the other teams you play will help the team get enough wins to play in the championship game. If your team does not make it to the championship game or loses the championship game, focus on how much they learned, how this has made them better players and that next year they will have another chance. Any recognition (i.e. trophy) that a team gets at the end of the year should be praised, and the emphasis should be on how what they learned throughout the season made this recognition possible. In this age group it is all about having fun and the pressure exerted on you to coach a winning team is minimal (in most cases). See the chapter on dealing with parents to learn how to handle those unfortunate situations where you have overzealous parents. Enjoy teaching these young athletes about the sport they are playing and whenever winning and losing enter into the picture, focus on how the more they practice and learn the more they will have the opportunity to win.

Winning Factor, 7-11 years old (20%)

Now that your players are getting older, their focus on winning may be intensifying. With this increased desire to win comes the disappointment of defeat. Undoubtedly in this age group, particularly at the upper end, there will be playoffs at the end of the year to determine the championship. Your players will show quite a bit of interest in this championship and certain players will exert their talents more than others in the quest to win it. It is important to keep egos in check. A coach who allows a tremendously gifted player to develop an inflated sense of ego is creating a disastrous situation, as this player's ego will continue to grow to the point that this player has no regard for those around him or her. Always make sure that you keep your players grounded by following the lessons from this book. That being said, during this stage it is permissible and even advised to start recognizing individual players. Most coaches like to have a "player of the game." In this age group never repeat the same player until all the players have been recognized as "player of the game." Make sure you keep a record of who has been selected. When making this recognition keep your focus on the hard work that made this recognition possible. Don't simply say, "Johnny scored the goal that won us the game; that is why he is the player of the game." The following is more appropriate: "Johnny always works hard at practice and it is because of this hard work that he was able to help us win the game by scoring the final goal." By recognizing individual players now, you are preparing them for the next level in which individual accolades become more prevalent. You could even pick a player who played just a few minutes, but whose hard work and great sprit propelled the team to be successful in the game.

In this age group it is also important to begin to more actively involve players in the win/loss record of the team. The best way to do this is by talking once a week about the team's record and their relative position to the first place team. There are two primary reasons for involving the team more in their record. First, it allows them to get excited and helps motivate them to work harder to achieve their goals. Second, if a player chooses to keep playing the sport they will move into age groups where the percentage of focus on winning will increase. A player who has not learned to cope with winning and losing may end up feeling like they were thrown into the deep end of the pool.

This is such an important age group to coach, as you are really starting to see players come into their own and show increasing interest in competitive sports. It is important that you really focus on the winning factor during this stage so that players who choose to continue to play will be better equipped to handle the increased demand for winning at the next levels.

Winning Factor, 12-14 years old (40%)

Now the focus on winning starts to build up and as a coach you must try really hard to create an environment where the quest for wins does not overshadow player development. In this age group some players choose to be on traveling teams that maintain challenging schedules and place a great deal of stock on winning. Not only are the players' expectations to win increasing, so are those of the parents (many of whom have invested a great deal of money in their child's sporting activities). One of the biggest problems with this age group is that their maturation level has not caught up with the pressures to win. As an EYC you are in a great position to change this often-harmful situation of over-competiveness and brutal schedules. It is important to keep everything in perspective during this stage. These athletes are still kids – the ultimate goal is about having fun and along the way developing their skills. The competitive nature of your players must be harnessed and then focused on developing the complete player. Use the advice provided in the chapters on the first two age groups and magnify these strategies to accommodate the increased focus on winning. At this point many of your players are going to be very concerned about their record in relation to the rest of the league. Use this concern to teach them how working as a team will help them continue to win. While it is still not advised that you keep formal individual stats, many of your players will probably be keeping track themselves. You can use this as a motivator for them to work hard towards their goals. Certain coaching scenarios may make stats a mainstay. This is okay – just always make sure you are keeping things in perspective. Remember the CEYC mantra: "Winning is something, but not everything." During this age group you are really beginning to embrace winning and allowing your players to be exposed to all the joys of winning and the disappointments of losing.

One of the biggest changes during this stage is that we feel it is allowable for a coach to show disappointment in your team's loss. Now, this does not mean we are advocating that you shout and scream at your team and tell them that they are all failures. Your disappointment should stem from the following two areas: 1) Your team showing less than their normal effort, and 2) You are human and when your team loses you are disappointed. The first reason may cause you to become upset. When your team gives a lackluster performance, you must temper your anger. In a situation like this, indicate to your team that you are displeased with their performance. However, do not elevate your voice to a shouting level. Encourage them to look within themselves to find out why they gave less than 100% and how they are going to improve their effort the next time. Remember, you are always guiding your players to improve and learn, and a situation like this is no different. While it may feel good to express your anger to the team it ultimately achieves nothing but motivation by fear. This type of motivation is not sustainable because it requires an ever-increasing level of intimidation from the coach.

Winning Factor 14-18 years old (60%)

For a youth coach this age group is the "big leagues." This is both a tremendously exciting group to coach and can also be quite stressful. Not only are you dealing with players' and parents' expectations to win, now you must deal with the school's expectations for a winning sports team. Many high school coaches lose their jobs because they are unable to produce a winning team. With all this pressure to win it can become quite easy for a coach to lose their cool and adopt a win at all costs mentality. For coaches in this situation it is important to take a step back and focus on the most important thing, the players and the tremendous opportunity you have to help them not only achieve their sports goals but enable them to gain insights that will benefit them throughout their lives. Some coaches even have the opportunity to coach players who will go on to play in college, perhaps even with a scholarship, and some coaches have the even rarer opportunity to coach players who go on to play professional sports. No mater what skill level of players you coach, it is a high probability that these young athletes have been involved with sports for some time. This is something to honor. These young men and women have chosen to stay active by involving themselves in sports. The focus on winning during this age group is quite dominant and will most likely have a constant presence on your team. In most situations players will be constantly aware of the team's record. It is best to embrace this awareness so that you can put perspective on how their effort is paying off, or if your team is struggling, how they can improve. A coach that ignores his or her team's record in front of the players is losing the opportunity to channel the players' emotions towards improving. Individual players' stats now come into focus and again this must also be embraced. However, it is important to make sure that your players are not obsessing over their stats. Therefore, you must lead by example and avoid going overboard with statistical analysis. Once a week updates are the perfect solution.

The most important point you can take home for coaching this age group is to temper your desire to win and focus on developing complete players. While this may be easier said than done, it is your mission as an EYC. If you focus on the complete player, winning will take care of itself.

The gradual process of introducing winning and losing into a player's sporting career allows for them to keep their focus on becoming a complete player by developing the four key areas of character development. Now that you have an understanding of how to introduce winning and losing across various age groups, we will use this knowledge to address the very important issue of playing time.

Playing Time

One of the most important issues you will deal with during this stage is playing time. If not dealt with properly, playing time can often put a strain on team unity. However, as an EYC coach you know all the hard work you put into establishing unity on your team will absorb most issues that arise from playing time. However, sometimes even the most unified teams can become divided. This most often occurs when the talent level on a team is not equally distributed; a team that has a several players that outshine the rest command more playing time because they play at such a high level. As an EYC coach you know that winning is not your only goal, so cutting back these players' playing time should not be too difficult…right? Well, this is true for coaches who are prepared. It is important to note that the CEYC is not suggesting that coaches allow every player equal playing time. In a perfect situation this would be the case. However, situations like this rarely arise – it is highly unlikely that the talent level on your team will be so even that allowing equal playing time will have no effect on your win/loss record. Most coaches are confronted with the reality that there are often great disparities in the abilities of the players on their team.

How then is a coach who has a responsibility to develop his or her players, maintain team unity, and win games able to effectively manage playing time? By "effectively" we don't simply mean plugging in certain players at the very end of a game when your team is winning by a wide margin. Even very young players can recognize when they are being put in to a game because their performance will have no bearing on the outcome. The following are strategies that a coach can utilize in order to effectively involve everyone on their team.

Strategies to Determine Playing Time

By the time your team plays their first game you should have a good idea of each of your players' strengths and weaknesses, because you have built your foundation as we suggested. With this knowledge you have determined which players maximize your teams chances of winning, and determined your starting line-up from these players. The CEYC finds no fault with this methodology. However, many coaches run into problems when they have no concrete strategy for including the other players in games. Simply following the strategy "I will work them in when I can" is not effective, and does not create strong team chemistry. Therefore, you must be well organized to effectively deal with playing time. Removing other variables from the equation (injury, fatigue, discipline, etc.), the ultimate reason a coach decides not to implement a player is because of his or her desire to win. By "benching" players with less talent a coach is maximizing a team's chance to win. Therefore, the more emphasis a coach places on winning the more likely certain players will sit on the bench. Now, as an EYC coach you are familiar with the "winning factor," which will help guide you in deciding how to fairly distribute playing time. For someone who coaches a team of six year-olds, deciding playing time is fairly straightforward: everyone plays equally because there is little emphasis placed on winning. At the next level, ages 7-11, it is more of the same but now the players who have higher talent levels can see a little more playing time. Where a coach has to start being more selective is at the 12 and above age range.

Let's use the 12-14 age range, where winning accounts for 40% of a coach's focus, to illustrate how a coach uses the winning factor to develop a playing time strategy. In order to highlight the EYC approach to playing time we will use a hypothetical model. Please note, this model is meant to illustrate how a coach can implement the concepts set forth by the CEYC. It is up to the coach to apply these principles to their individual team. In Appendix B there is a blank template that coaches can use to formulate their own playing time strategy.

The following model is of a 12-14 boy's basketball team. The team is composed of 10 players: a, b, c, d, e, f, g, h, i, j. The team's talent level is as follows:

> *High Talent (ht): a*
> *Above Average Talent (aat): b, c, d*
> *Average Talent (at): e, f, g, and h*
> *Below Average Talent (bat): i, j*

Following the winning factor, a coach would place 40% emphasis on winning. Therefore, for 13 minutes a coach would go with their "max lineup" (a, b, c, d, e). These five players represent the highest talent levels on the team and therefore, all things considered, give the team the maximum chance of winning. It is up to the individual coach to determine how to implement the players within this 13 minute time frame. Some coaches may put this lineup out there for the first 13 minutes of the game. Others might start this lineup for 6 minutes, then begin to phase in other players, and then for the last 6 minutes use the max lineup again. This brings us to the next point: following the Winning Factor Model, a coach would have 19 minutes to utilize the players on his or her bench. The focus during these 19 minutes is to make sure that every player is utilized. This utilization is not an afterthought as is often the case when implementing the less talented players. During these 19 minutes, when a coach is focusing on utilizing all the players on their team, the coach does not have to put in a lineup that is composed solely of the less talented players (i.e. f, g, h, i, j). The key is that you are making a concerted effort to utilize all the players; blending them in with your more talented players is fine. The percentages and time frames are meant to give you a framework to work off of and are not absolute guidelines. As a coach you should seek to adhere as closely as possible to the recommendations put forth by the winning factor model. However, certain situations may make adjustments necessary. The bottom line is that you must get away from the mentality that "I will play Jimmy later" and give no thought to when "later" will occur.

Of course, the above example can be utilized in any sport and at any level of the winning factor. A high school baseball coach using a 60% winning factor would, for a seven inning game, use his or her max lineup for four innings and the alternative lineup for three innings. Now, depending on your team size and time constraints you may not be able to utilize all the players from your alternative lineup. The key to the above model is to make sure that you have a strategy for implementing all your players and that this strategy is not always dependent on winning. The percentages and allotted times are only meant to be a guide in helping you distribute playing time on your team.

A coach must also avoid favoritism when making decisions about playing time. Many coaches, particularly volunteer coaches, have a child on the team they are coaching. It is important to treat your child no differently from any other player on the team. Furthermore, you will undoubtedly find yourself looking more favorably upon certain players than others; you must temper these feelings with what is fair to everyone. Always treat your players equally. Now that the winning factor and playing time have been addressed, the focus will turn to describing special considerations during this stage.

Developmental Skills in Winning and Losing

The winning factor provided you with the framework on how to gradually implement the concept of winning across various age groups. As we enter into our discussion of developmental skills we will talk about the relation of winning and losing to player confidence. An EYC coach uses wins to build confidence and preserves confidence in spite of losses.

One of the greatest joys an athlete can experience is to win a championship. One only has to observe a team for a brief moment after a big win to see the confidence exhibited by each player. Winning is an affirmation of all the hard work and dedication a team put forth. When your team wins it is important to use the win to build the confidence of your players. Before you give out individual accolades, make sure you compliment the whole team for a job well done. Once you have addressed the whole team, call out several individuals who had outstanding performances. When you are addressing these individual players make sure you emphasize how their hard work was critical to their success and how their ability to work with fellow teammates was instrumental. Close your address to the team by, once again, complimenting the team as a whole. Undoubtedly there were mistakes made during the game. However, unless these mistakes jeopardized the safety of your players or displayed a lack of sportsmanship, it is best not to address them right after a win. Once your team is gone make note of the areas that need improvement and set out to work on these areas during the next practice. There is nothing that can deflate a player's confidence quicker that hearing a coach break down the things they did incorrectly right after a big win. A win goes a long way in building a player's confidence. This gain in confidence will pay a lot more dividends than nitpicking through the details. Furthermore, after a game you usually don't have the time to give problem-solving these mistakes the attention they can be given in the next practice. Celebrate your win and leave the coaching for the upcoming practice.

While wins can do wonders for confidence, losses can do the exact opposite. Unless you are one of the select few who coach an undefeated team you will have to deal with losses. While no coach likes to lose, you must embrace your losses as an opportunity to learn and grow as a team. Your number one priority is to preserve your players' confidence. If you coach a team that seldom loses this can be quite easy. For coaches in this group: after the game, make sure you tell the team you are proud of their effort and recognize those players who excelled. After a loss, unlike after a win, it is okay to point out the areas the team needs to work on and how you will accomplish this at the next practice. Make sure you are not being negative and do not fixate on the mistakes. It is important that you assure your team that the next practice is going to be great because they are going to have an opportunity to improve and grow as players.

For those who coach a team that loses more games than they win it can be tremendously difficult to keep players' confidence levels high. The above approach still applies, but you are going to have to dig deep to find ways to keep your players upbeat. For coaches in this situation it is important to focus on the overall aim of the EYC. Remind yourself and your players of all the positive aspects of their participation in sports. Point out to your players that through hard work they will improve. Remind them to focus on the fun of playing, being with their teammates, and playing well.

Another area that coaches should be prepared to handle is individual players who are struggling. Please read the following hypothetical situation and then write a short response.

John is a nine-year-old boy who plays on a football team. Whenever John drops a pass he cries and gets extremely down on himself. John's coach is concerned that John's behavior is not only bad for him but also the team. The coach is worried that the other players will make fun of John and tease him for being a "baby." How should the coach handle this situation? Write your response on the lines below.

_____

_____

_____

_____

_____

_____

_____

_____

_____

_____

_____

We recommend handling the above situation in the following manner. This is when you draw on all the concepts set forth in this book. If you are following the methods outlined herein you can be confident that you are doing everything in your power to create a positive environment for your team and are promoting self-confidence among your players.

The main thing you want to focus on after you have assessed your coaching style is the individual player. Ask yourself these questions: Is the player afraid? Does the player continually show a lack of confidence during games and practices? How does the player interact with his or her teammates? What is the status of the player's home life?

Is the player afraid? This is a fairly straightforward question and is one that is typically easy to answer. When you observe this player, does he interact frequently with his fellow teammates or does he sit by himself on the bench and often avoid interaction? Let's say our football player from the above example is shy. Many children at this age are shy, as they are still developing their social skills. In this case John's shyness may be causing him to feel embarrassed and frustrated when he drops a pass, and this embarrassment and frustration is leading him to cry. As a coach the best way to handle this, taking into account that you are already following all the guidelines of the EYC coaching model, is to focus on team building exercises. You must promote interaction between the players and allow them to become more comfortable around each other. Remember, it is never acceptable to force something on a player and make them feel uncomfortable. Team building is a gradual process and some players take longer to embrace the concepts. Get John more involved with the team and his shyness will soon dissipate.

If addressing the shyness does not do the trick, then look at John's confidence and self-esteem levels. In observing John you notice that he is always the last one to volunteer for practice drills and he appears to show no concern when he is not playing. Unlike the other players on the team, John seems content not to play. Chapter 12 will deal with self-esteem and confidence building; this is where you should go in order to get the specifics on how to help players dealing with these issues. However, for the purposes of addressing the above situation let's focus on how low levels of self-esteem and confidence might be causing John to cry after dropping a pass and how boosting his self-confidence can remedy the situation. From John's actions during games and practices it is clear that his belief in his ability to receive passes while playing is limited. The coach must focus on ways to build John's confidence. This process does not happen right away and patience must be maintained. Focus on **small victories** with players like John. If John drops a pass, praise him for running a good route. Always look at the positive and direct your praise towards these aspects. Please refer to Chapter 12 for more strategies on how to build confidence and self-esteem.

Now that we have gotten John to come out of his shell more and display confidence a noticeable improvement is taking place. However, there is still something missing. The final situation to consider is the player's home life. This is a very delicate area and unless you are a trained counselor there is only so much you can do.

Later chapters will deal with special situations. However, for now the important point to take home is recognition. If you recognize that a player is having difficulty at home it can shed light on why a player is struggling and allow you to be sensitive to their individual needs. It is important to remember that it is never okay to show extreme levels of favoritism to players. Just because John may be having trouble at home does not mean he should be excused from practice drills. What his trouble at home means is that you must be prepared for mood swings, and you should do everything in your power to boost his confidence and have him interact with the team. If you are uncertain about the degree of the player's troubles at home, seek the advice of professionals who are equipped to handle situations of this nature. Chapter 13 will assist you in finding help.

The above paragraphs break down how you can assess a situation involving a struggling player and the possible steps to remedy the situation. It is always important to be honest with yourself. If a situation makes you uncomfortable or is outside your abilities, seek help. Furthermore, always make sure you are not focusing all your energy on one individual situation at the cost of losing focus on the team as a whole.

Healthy Lifestyle

Now that we have addressed developmental skills during stage four, let's turn our focus to how to promote a healthy lifestyle. During this stage your players will be quite busy, particularly those playing on school teams. Commonly, when individuals are busy they ignore healthy eating and sleeping practices. As an EYC coach it is important that you stop this unhealthy cycle. Talk to your team about the importance of getting enough sleep (nine hours for young athletes) and how it will help to replenish and repair their bodies for better performance. Make sure your team is aware of how critical a balanced diet is to their athletic performance and how they must maintain this diet even when their schedule is demanding.

Some coaches may be in a situation in which parents bring food for players to enjoy after a game or there is the occasional visit to an ice cream shop. These are important treats and they should not be looked down upon. It is important to find balance with these treats.

Constantly having donuts and soda is not a good idea. Conversely, carrot sticks and hummus all the time is also counterproductive. Coordinate with parents to bring a variety of snacks and focus on keeping a nice balance. If you have cupcakes make sure there is juice or if there is soda make sure there are bagels. Keeping the children you coach excited about sports and a healthy lifestyle is incredibly important for helping them stay healthy throughout the rest of their lives.

Sportsmanship

In the previous three stages you laid the groundwork for sportsmanship by addressing its importance during practices. Now you get to witness the sportsmanship displayed by your team as they encounter other teams. When a team shows a lack of sportsmanship it is a serious issue and you must act accordingly. If an individual player is the culprit, address the issue with player as soon as possible. It is important that the whole team is aware of why this player's conduct is unacceptable; just make sure you are not making a grandiose display. If the whole team shows a lack of sportsmanship, address the team directly and explain to them that their actions are unacceptable and will not be tolerated. It is important to be stern in your address, but make sure you are not yelling. If your team continues to show a lack of sportsmanship indicate to them that playing is a privilege and that if their actions continue they will cease to play. Unfortunately, in many situations, the lack of sportsmanship displayed by a team stems from the coach.

To illustrate this point let's examine the following coaching situation, in which a basketball coach calls a timeout to talk to their team, which is on a 10-0 run.

Great job guys! You are really pounding these guys! Let's keep pounding them down until they can't stand it anymore.

In this exchange the coach is setting forth an aggressive metaphor about the other team in order to motivate his own team. How are the players on this team supposed to display sportsmanship when their coach is talking down the other team? After the game, are the players simply supposed to flip a switch and shake the hands of the other team at the end of the game? The above coach's answer would be yes!

And this typically does happen. However, a seed is being planted in these young men and women's minds that it is okay to have views that lack sportsmanship. As a coach it is your job to motivate your players and there is nothing wrong with getting your players in a huddle, cheering them on and pumping them up. The key point here is not to motivate your team by debasing the other team, as this will promote bad sportsmanship on your team. Remember, your players are not adults and many of them lack the maturity to prevent your debasing comments from affecting their attitude towards the other team. Always show respect towards the other team even if they do not extend the same courtesy.

Team Building

All the work you did in the three previous stages will pay dividends during the team building stage. By the time your team begins to play games they should be very comfortable with each other and be able to work well together. The emphasis you placed on team unity and equal treatment will become evident as you observe your team working together and communicating.

Many sports are very physical and often involve contact. These aggressive plays look very impressive and teams cheer wildly at the site of them (i.e. big football hits). However, the reality of these "big hits" is that they can cause serious damage to the other player. Recent research is pointing to the dangers of sports concussions and how many warning signs have been neglected. The old mantra of "he got his bell rung, he will be fine in a minute" is no longer acceptable. While these "big hits" are often legal plays and are done with no malice, you should not advocate to your team to cheer at the sight of potential harm to another player. When a player is hit hard and appears to be injured, your team should remain silent and you should immediately go offer assistance. If the player's condition is only temporary your players should clap as the player walks off the field. If the injured player's situation does not get better and outside medical assistance is needed, have your players remain quiet. It is important to make sure that your players are not joking around, as the opposing team is going to be very concerned about the player and even a few laughs can be taken the wrong way. At the end of the game encourage your players to check in on the player's condition. The EYC advocates that every game end with the teams lining up and shaking each other's hands.

The next chapter will deal with the end of the season and how a coach can help prepare his or her team for the next level. This was a long chapter that dealt with a lot of heavy-duty issues. One important point to always keep in mind is that you must never abandon your ethical principles in the quest to win.

Keywords:
Working on the Interior
Win At All Costs Model
-No-Score Leagues
-Winning Factor
-Perception of Winning

Questions:
1) Why does the CEYC advocate less of a focus on winning?
2) Why is playing time less of an issue at the younger levels of youth sports?
3) (True or False) Confidence is one of the areas most directly touched by winning.
4) Why do some coaches abandon EYC principles during games?
5) At what level is playing time the most difficult to determine?
6) List the four age groups of the Winning Factor.
7) Describe how a coach utilizes the Winning Factor to determine playing time.
8) (True or False) Lack of sportsmanship often stems from the coach.
9) Why is it important that players do not cheer at big hits?

Suggested Activities:
1) Fill out Appendix B to help determine how you will distribute playing time on your team.

Chapter 9
Stage Five: Laying the Field

This chapter will focus on how a coach should handle the end of the season. In the five stages of player development this is the fifth and final stage. In this stage you are **laying the field** or, put more concretely, you are helping set the tone for your players' future athletic endeavors. Like playing time, this is an often-neglected aspect of a coach's planning process. Many coaches are so busy during the season that they neglect to consider how they will part ways with their team at the end of the season. Much like the planning you put into the pre-season meeting, a little bit of preparation goes a long way at the end of the season. You have spent a great deal of time with your team and in many cases you will not see your players again on a regular basis. You want to make sure you are ending your season on a positive note and not simply saying "bye" after the last play is completed.

Some coaches may question why this is a stage in player development. The reason it is a stage of development is because how you end a season can be critically important to the perception your players have of sports. A coach who ends the season by simply saying "its been fun" or worse yet, saying something negative such as "you ruined your season by losing that last game," is influencing a player's perception of their participation in sports. Players remember the things that occur at the end of the season best. Psychologists refer to this as the **recency effect**. Leaving your players with positive feelings can go a long way in encouraging future participation. This is of particular importance at the younger levels, where not only is the recency effect more prevalent, but a player has fewer positive experiences to absorb the potential negative experiences. Telling a group of seven year-olds that they had a bad season can potentially turn them away from that sport or, worse yet, all sports for the rest of their lives. Therefore, it is best to have a plan for how you are going to end your season on a positive note.

As the season comes to a close you will have a clearer picture of how your team stands from a win/loss perspective. Did you win more than you lost? Are you going to a playoff situation? Is your team in a position to win a championship? All these are questions to consider when planning your end of year strategy. For those who are coaching a team that wins a championship, the end of season planning is pretty straightforward. However, for those who coach teams that had less than stellar performances, how to end a season on a positive note may not be so obvious or easy.

The first thing a coach can do is separate the last game from the last meeting. The last game refers to the last official game a team plays and the last meeting refers to the last gathering a team has, which is often a end of year party. At the end of the last game it is recommended that the coach gather his or her team together and congratulate them on a great season. Applaud all the hard work they put into the season and encourage them to continue their athletic pursuits. It is important to not only encourage them to continue in the sport they are currently engaged in but invite them to consider other sports. All too often in modern youth sports there is pressure to "specialize" in one sport. This can be detrimental to the development of kids' motor skills (particularly for younger athletes). Furthermore, research is pointing out that specialization in sports can increase the likelihood of injury as certain muscles are over-utilized, causing an imbalance in the muscular system. While you want to and should encourage your players to continue playing the sport you coach, it is important to not go overboard and set a tone that demands that your players continue playing only that sport. Make sure you have a few examples from throughout the season of why you are proud of the team. After you have addressed the team, take the whole team over to the parents and thank the parents. In the chapter later on Dealing With Parents we will discuss in more detail how to effectively communicate with parents. However, for right now the most important thing to keep in mind is to be genuine when talking with the parents and involve the whole team in your expression of gratitude. The most important thing to remember during this final after-game meeting is to point out how much fun you had coaching the team. At the end of the meeting invite everyone from the team to an end of season party. By now you should be somewhat familiar with your players' and parents' schedules, so use this knowledge to determine the date for the party. If possible, let everyone know the date of the party before the final game. Remember, it is usually not possible to pick a date that satisfies everybody's schedule. Just pick a day that maximizes the possibility of attendance. Also, don't just rely on the school or the league to hold a party. Schedule your own. It pays big dividends.

The focus of the party should be on having fun and sharing memories from the season. It is important not to make this a recruitment session for playing on next year's team or another coach's team. This party is a reward for a job well done. As such, serving indulgent food is not a problem; however, subtly point out the fact that this "feast" is because of their hard work. Let's say it one more time, because it is an important point: this party is not a recruitment tool for next year's team! Below is a list of things to consider before the final game of the year.

-Ending on a positive note
-Emphasizing fun
-Encouraging participation in sports in general
-Remembering great moments throughout the season
-Setting a date for the end of year party

The Five Stages of Player Development in Perspective

Now that the final stage of player development is complete and you have been exposed to all five stages of player development, it is important to understand that the five stages are cyclical in nature. As soon as a player starts another year/season/sport, the five stages start all over again, and if you are able to coach the same players the following year you would go through all fives stages again. As you hone your skills as a coach you will be able to determine how to progress through the stages of development. It is always a safer bet to move too slowly than too fast. Whether you have coached a player before or not you are always building a new stadium each time you start a new season.

The next section will deal with special considerations in youth coaching. If you have not yet done so, turn to Appendix A to view a sample coaching plan, which shows you the five stages of player development in action. This will give you a summary of how all five stages work throughout the season.

Keywords:
-Laying the field
-Recency Effect

Study Questions:
1) Why is the end of the season an often-neglected time?
2) Why is stage five a stage of player development?
3) Why is leaving your players with positive feelings particularly important for younger players?
4) Why do you separate the last game from the last meeting?
5) (True or False) You should encourage your players to play other sports.
6) (True or False) You should use the end of year party to recruit players.
7) (True or False) The Five Stages of Player Development are cyclical in nature.

Suggested Activities:
1) Create your own end of year checklist.

Part III

Special Considerations

Chapter 10
Maximizing Your Effectiveness with Young Athletes: A Developmental Perspective

Section Author: Dr. John Mayer

Guiding young athletes is a complex endeavor. Coaches, volunteers, and professionals in all fields of sports become frustrated when trying to lead young people. It is an age-old problem that adults attempt to apply a successful method used on adults and assume that these same methods will work just as successfully on young people. I addressed this issue early in my career when I called attention to the special needs of teenagers regarding substance abuse. Young people's needs in substance abuse detection and treatment were not being met because professionals were applying successful techniques from the adult alcohol and substance abuse field and assumed that these techniques would work just as well on youth. The problem was that these successful techniques were not built upon the developmental needs and capacities of youth. Thus, not only couldn't young people relate to these techniques, they did not meet their specific needs.

The field of sports finds itself in the same position. A large part of the dilemma for sports professionals is that young people have changed in their attitudes and abilities significantly in the last sixty years, yet sports professionals approach young people as if they are still in the mid-1900s. Young people are increasingly being turned off by adults leading them in sports because they just can't relate to the techniques used to guide them. Again, this phenomenon of leadership is not unique to sports. Many professional fields employ techniques that I would term **'revolving-door' techniques**. For example, it is well known in medicine that physicians employ techniques that they learned in residency, then teach these techniques to new physicians and so forth and so on. My book, *Family Fit*, chronicled how many of our favorite eating habits have their origins in a society that was agriculturally based. People's lives were dominated by manual labor and physical activity, thus they had higher caloric needs. Change is slow. The problem in sports is not with the X's and O's. The techniques of playing sports have evolved tremendously. The problem lies with leadership techniques that have no grounding in the developmental stages of youth.

Let's review what we know about child and adolescent development and offer suggestions on how these techniques can be applied to sports success. Let's also assume that our young athletes begin to participate in sports at five years of age. This is a convenient starting age because the same leadership considerations apply for those coaching kids under five.

Ages 5 to 7

From age 5 to 7, children are very heavily into the **'Me' stage of overall development**. The concept of peers or others in the world is a vague one at best. Children at this age are reconciling themselves with the world around them by building skills that allow them to understand that people and things can be depended on and trusted. They are also beginning to learn how to control impulses, obey rules and live with an internal sense of order and regularity. They still struggle cognitively with connecting their behavior with consequences, so when parents discipline children at this age it is hard for the child to "generalize" consequences to other behaviors. This is frustrating for parents.

In sports, consider these same dynamics. Young athletes at this age are highly distracted. They will impulsively leave the field of play or court and do what they feel like. This action is not rebellion, it is being a child. Don't treat it as defiance. Firmly and respectfully guide the child back to the task at hand. Remember that at this age patience on their part is very weak. Keep practices and even games short and very, very concrete. Children at this age are not 'stringing' directions (game plays, rules, techniques) together to establish a system. They can best follow minute, careful, circumscribed directions. If you keep the field of play small, there will be less chance of distraction and departure from the game.

Ages 7 to 11

From age 7 to 11, young people begin to be aware of their peers more and develop increasing consideration of the feelings and needs of their peers. Further, peer relationships begin to be more important. They move away from depending on their parents and the adults around them as the only influence on their life and actions. The beginnings of bullying and teasing behaviors are seen more as the opinions of others are now more important. 5th and 6th grade is a heightened time for bullying and teasing. Although they are still cognitively in a stage where concrete thinking dominates, they increasingly obtain the ability to string or chain experiences together. They can maintain the rules of games and follow through with rules and structure. People, objects, rules, and structure gain permanence to them. They trust more and are better able to control their impulses. They can respond more to consequences, though these consequences have to be immediate and be specific to them.

In sports, techniques such as "If you don't behave at practice you won't start on Saturday" just don't have an effect. Such consequences are simply too far in the future. Similarly, giving players profound statements about doing things for the good of the team, etc., are wasted. Athletes at this age are still in the 'Me' stage of social relations. Coaches are often tricked at this age by a young athlete's abilities because parents typically get more involved in their child's sports. For example, a coach may use a future-oriented technique and think it works, but what is really happening is that the parent is constantly reminding and maybe brow-beating the child at home about the consequence, so it is staying uppermost in the child's mind. In effect, the coach is actually training the parent(s) more than the young athlete. The sport has to continue to be fun and have positive value for the child for them to maintain interest and enthusiasm. The theme for them is: What have you done for me lately?

Ages 12 to 14

From age 12 to 14, peers become even more important, but parents still remain the dominant influence on young people. Young people at this age are still in "right and wrong," black and white methods of thinking about the world, or as Piaget called it, the cognitive stage of concrete operations. Interest and activity directed towards "romantic relationships" takes a center stage at this age. One of the first migrations away from sports participation occurs as other life interests arrive in the child's awareness. Along with sexual attraction to others, there are video games, cell phones, texting, Facebook, music – all kinds of social goodies that take interest away from sports. Failure becomes another fuel for migration away from sports. Prior to this age the inability to perform in sports was not often a perceived deficit in the young athlete. The recognition of failure is both a cognitive development and a dimension of sports in society. Prior to age 12, kids play sports with this same narcissistic, or "Me" outlook. Now, at this age, they can perceive how others perform, and they can realize how they stack up against other players on their team, because social awareness is building and becoming more acute. The young athlete is increasingly measuring him- or herself against others. This social judgment may result in frustration, sadness, and withdrawal in the young athlete. The result is that they want to quit. It is still important at this age to emphasize the individual rewards of sports participation.

Age 15 to 17

From age 15 to 17, social life expands even more greatly. Dating, driving, more liberal recreation hours and other adult-like privileges increase. Thinking about the true feelings of others and developing empathy and concern for social good is now developing. The young person is actively moving away from a "Me" orientation to thinking and empathizing with the feelings and needs of others. The good of the team now has more meaning. Techniques that emphasize the good of the whole group have some power in the teenager's life. But, adult-like temptations are very powerful as well. One of the largest migrations away from sports participation occurs during these years. The good news here is that those players who stay with their sport are typically those who have the most commitment and internal motivation.

One important feature of teenage development to consider is that teenage maturity is very unpredictable. Some teens will develop faster than others and vice versa. The paradox for some adults leading teens in sports is that some of the techniques they employ that are not age-appropriate may be effective with the teens they are guiding because they are precocious and their cognitive growth can absorb and thrive under them. A common dilemma is that some players "get it," but the majority don't. What's going on? What's going on is that they are teens, and teenage maturity is not uniform across any group of adolescents participating in any activity, let alone sports.

The guidelines set down here apply to the majority of teens. Another factor to consider regarding the precariousness of teenage development is intellectual capability. Teenagers of higher intellectual capability generally will mature faster than those of more limited intellectual ability. Adults who lead teens in sports must understand this wide discrepancy in ability across typical teenagers.

Age 18 to 22

For the majority of young adults in this age range their cognitive and social development has advanced such that they are fully into the **'We' stage of social cognition**. Young people this age thrive on thinking about the good of the group and the by-products of group efforts. Teamwork and sportsmanship are idealized and embraced. This is not to say that certain players won't be selfish and narcissistic, but these will be expressions of their own personality deficits and not necessarily by-products of their developmental stage.

Importantly, during this period the young person can fully appreciate and look forward to the future. Prior to this age young people were largely concerned with the here and now. It is very difficult to motivate younger athletes to look at the long-term benefits of their efforts. Now, at this age future rewards are understandable, even desirable for the athlete.

Most of us are aware that it is at this age when the young person is beginning to consider their place in society and to contemplate, even plan their role as an adult. This is the well-known quest for identity.

Being an athlete can be very beneficial to this quest. Athletics give the young person meaning and purpose. It is for this reason that ancient methods of negative reinforcement, insults, and punitive techniques are particularly harmful to the athlete at this age. Identity builds more successfully by positive reinforcement of the self-concept that the young athlete is building. Sure, some athletes may show a positive response to the primitive methods of decades past, but I would maintain that these responses are a result of competitiveness and not the primitive motivational techniques. The problem with these **negative motivational styles** is that they are very short-lived for the athlete. The athlete will respond with short bursts of performance under these techniques, but over the long haul (or a full season) the athlete will fail. This is because of the cognitive and social maturity of the athlete at this age. There are effective methods for motivating young athletes at this age and at all the ages discussed in this chapter. We'll examine these techniques, but first let's consider effective techniques for communicating with young people, based on the developmental knowledge outlined above. These techniques can be used in conjunction with the previously discussed techniques in Chapter 2.

Special Tips for Communicating with Young Athletes:

Establish respect. Kids know you are an adult; don't try to be a buddy or the cool dude coach. Kids have tremendous "lie-dar" and will see right through communication techniques that present you as anything other than who you are as an adult and a leader for them.

Listen. I mean really listen. Take an interest in their lives. Remember that the things that are important in their lives might not seem like such a big deal to you, but for them these things are nuclear bombs exploding all around them. Put yourself in their shoes – don't look at their life like an adult. Picture life as it presents itself to them. Remember that they are experiencing many things for the first time and they are not going to act as YOU would.

Watch your body language. Don't do goofy things like squatting down to their level or patting them on the head, etc. Again, they know you are an adult, bigger than they are, and it's odd if you talk with kid slang or baby talk. Always make eye contact and talk directly to them, not ABOUT them in front of other adults.

Model communication. Children and young people learn best by seeing how you communicate with others. Talk to all those around you in the same respectful, empathetic way you want others to talk to you. No yelling, abusive language or profanity. No teasing, no sarcasm, and don't lose your temper.

Empower young people. Make their ideas and opinions worthy by taking them into consideration. No question is a bad question. Seek out their advice. It is great for them to hear, "What do you think we should do in this situation?"

Be patient. Young people are not finished products; they just haven't learned many communication skills yet. This doesn't make them *unsocialized*, disadvantaged, or deficient, it makes them KIDS. Don't expect young people to be perfect or to do things how you would.

Special Tips on Motivating Young People:

Attitude-Attitude-Attitude. Motivating children and youth starts with the attitude you present to them. Your attitude should be one of kindness and teaching. You are giving something to the kids. Your attitude should convey this service orientation. Be positive; supply the energy in the relationship with the child.

Surround young people with motivation. Use positive affirmations liberally and often. A good resource for these are the affirmations researched by the Search Institute in Minnesota. They call these affirmations "the 40 Developmental Assets." These forty assets are social actions that this foundation's research has shown are important in the healthy development of a young person. Take a look at them; they can be valuable references for ways you can approach a child with affirmations.

<u>The best motivator of all is verbal praise from an adult</u>. Verbal praise given face-to-face by an adult beats other motivators such as money, gifts, material rewards of all types and even peer accolades. Use verbal praise liberally with young people.

<u>Praise effort and not accomplishment</u>. Affirming the effort a young person puts into an athletic endeavor is more motivating than affirming the accomplishment. Accomplishment is the result of so many intangible and tangible factors that are not in the sole control of the child – the competitor's skills and resources, a lucky bounce, mistakes, bad calls, etc. – such that the effort a young person puts into an athletic activity is much more ripe for motivation than the accomplishment. Further, accomplishment is often translated by the young person as praise for their native ability or potential and this ability/potential can be transitory. When you praise effort, you are emphasizing skill development over results, and you will see huge growth in the young athlete from this emphasis.

<u>Don't crush them over mistakes</u>. Use mistakes as the ultimate teaching moment. It is commonly acknowledged that we learn best from our mistakes. Capitalize on these opportunities for the child to learn.

<u>Don't confuse lack of motivation with lack of ability</u>. Assess a youth's abilities honestly and motivate them with all the concepts listed here, within what their abilities allow. This is where praising effort is especially important. You are motivating the less capable athlete with praise even though the results of their efforts are not accomplishing as much as the more talented athlete.

<u>Sarcasm and negative motivation has no place in the leadership of today's young athletes</u>. That says it all.

<u>Internal Motivators are more powerful than External Motivators</u>. Many adults believe that by being dominant over the young athlete, they will perform better. Fear techniques, yelling, berating the young athlete, are all examples of external motivators. These motivators are seductive. They can appear to work effectively temporarily, especially

while the adult leader is present to apply the external motivation. However, they are transitory because if you take the external motivator away, the young athlete quickly becomes unmotivated, even rebellious. It is important to note here that for athletes at the youngest ages as listed here (5-7 and 7-11), external motivators do work better than those that are internally-oriented. This is because the cognitive and social development of the child athlete at these ages is not advanced enough to develop internal motivation sufficiently. This occurs as a result of all the developmental conditions outlined above. Children at these ages love to play for play's sake, but to expect them to have an allegiance to the 'sport' is shortsighted. They are just children who love to play.

In summary, the following general principles will result in great leadership of young athletes across all ages:

- Be consistent
- Be respectful
- Always impose boundaries, structure and discipline
- Be empathetic
- Communicate effectively
- Listen
- Use affirmations
- Set high standards but realize that young people will fail
- Always be a model and a team player yourself
- Base your leadership on their developmental capabilities, not on the adult standards by which you were led

Keywords:
Revolving Door Techniques
"Me" Stage of Overall Development
"We" Stage of Social Cognition
Negative Motivational Styles

Questions:
1) (True or False) You should use the same motivational techniques with children as with adults.
2) Why do children become turned off from sports?

3) How should a coach react if a five-year-old refuses to play?

4) (True or False) Athletes ages 7 to 11 are still in the "me" stage of development.

5) List three interests that develop during the 12 to 14 age group and which may distract youth from sports.

6) (True or False) At age 12 players begin to compare themselves to other players.

7) (True or False) Some teens will develop faster than others.

8) Why are negative motivational techniques not successful?

9) List and explain three tips for communicating with young athletes.

10) List and explain three tips for motivating young people.

Chapter 11
Yelling as a Form of Communication

Unfortunately, for some, yelling has become synonymous with coaching. In fact some people view yelling as part of coaching and if a coach is not "yelling" they are not doing their job. A coach who sits back and calmly directs his or her team can be seen as aloof and lacking the desire to win. However, a coach who is in his or her players' faces and yelling all the time is seen as a great motivator who cares if his or her team wins. Why do people feel this way? How can we change this strong belief in yelling? This chapter seeks to answer these questions and provide the Ethical Youth Coach with the tools to stop the vicious yelling cycle.

We hope all our nuggets of wisdom are going to stick with you throughout your coaching career, but if there is only one point that you take from this book, hopefully it will be from this chapter. The Center for Ethical Youth Coaching advocates that yelling is only acceptable when a player's safety is in jeopardy, and that furthermore this is not really yelling but rather raising your voice in the face of a dangerous situation. Yelling at a player who fails is not acceptable. Yelling at a player who is not responsive is not acceptable. One important distinction that must be made is between "yelling" and "cheering." **Yelling** occurs when an emotional state, typically anger, is aroused in a coach due to players' actions. **Cheering** occurs when a coach is loudly encouraging a player. Cheering is a form of positive reinforcement and is critical to being a successful coach. The following are examples of a yelling coach and a cheering coach.

Yelling:
Coach A's little league baseball team is down to their last out and in order to win the game they need a hit. Coach A calls the player about to bat over and loudly tells the player that he better get a hit or else the team is going to be doing a lot of running after the game, because the team they are playing is horrible and does not deserve to beat them.

Cheering:
Coach B's little league baseball team is down to their last out and in order to win the game they need a hit. Coach B calls the player about to bat over and tells him he knows he is going to do great and to trust all the drills they have done in practice. While the player is walking to the batting circle Coach B loudly says to the player "You're the man" and "I know you are going to do great."

In addition to yelling at the player what are the other Ethical Youth Coaching violations of Coach A? List them here:

1) _____

2) _____

One of the violations you should have picked up on right away is that the coach threatens the team with running as a punishment. As was stated earlier, running is never an acceptable form of punishment. The other violation is that Coach B talks poorly of the other team. In the yelling example the coach's posturing is not only intimidating to the player, but also threatens to create a negative association with running. The belittling of another team shows the player that it is okay to talk down other teams. A coach who engages in this style of coaching will soon have players who complain every time they have to run, and who, whenever they encounter players from another team, will tell them that "your team stinks." Is this the type of players you want to create?

Coach B, on the other hand, perfectly embodies how to cheer on your players. Not only does he try to inspire his players with positive statements, he also creates a correlation between hard work and success. Hard work paying off is the essence of the Ethical Youth

Coaching Model. While most players won't make a living playing sports, the lesson that hard work will help you succeed is something that benefits everyone.

The one common theme in both of the above coaches' approaches is the elevation of their voice. All the casual onlooker (e.g., a parent who is chatting with the person next to them while watching the game) may see is a coach raising their voice, making it possible that the distinction between Coach A's and Coach B's messages will get lost. An environment could be created in which both cheering and yelling become acceptable and even expected. However, as an ethical youth coach it is your duty to stop this cycle and create an environment in which yelling is not an acceptable form of communication.

Many coaches are quick to point out that sometimes yelling is necessary to motivate a stubborn player or to discipline an unruly player. In other words, "yelling works." To some extent these coaches are correct. Yelling does arouse an emotional response in players, causing them to react almost instantly. However, these reactions slow as players become habituated to the yelling, forcing the coach to increase the intensity of the yelling. As a result, players act in response to intimidation and not motivation. The immediate human response to yelling is to immediately become defensive, shut down, and therefore not hear the message. Yelling simply does not accomplish anything you intend. Furthermore, some coaches begin to cross the line and enter into the area of verbal abuse. Let's take a look at a classic scenario and two different approaches to handling the situation.

Yelling Approach:

Coach A's soccer team is working on drills during a practice and the coach calls her players over for a demonstration. Whenever the coach gathers the players together she expects them to run over. One of the players walks slowly to the demonstration, and when the coach yells for the player to run the player yells back "I'm tired." The coach immediately flies off the handle and yells to the player that she is lazy and worthless! After yelling at the player she tells the player to start running.

Now let's take the same scenario and utilize a non-yelling approach.

Non-Yelling Approach:

Coach B calls out to the walking player in a firm but non-hostile way, "remember, on this team we run to see a demonstration." Upon hearing the "I'm tired" response, the coach calmly waits until the player makes it to the demonstration and asks the player why she is tired. When the player offers no valid reason for being tired and the coach sees no physical evidence of exhaustion, the coach indicates to the player that only players who are motivated will play in games and if this player continues to disobey team rules they will lose playing time.

Coach A's approach is to yell at the player and then punish them by running. Coach A chooses to have an emotional response that, while directed at a specific player, is observed by the whole team. Coach A is showing his or her players that it is okay to "fly off the handle" to remedy a situation. This is not acceptable behavior to model for young athletes. In contrast, Coach B calmly assesses the situation and makes the player aware of the consequences of not following team policies. It is important to note that Coach B first **assesses the situation** and then addresses the issue. What if the player really was exhausted and not just being lazy? One need only turn to the media to see stories of coaches pushing their players to the limit, with disastrous consequences. As a coach you must always be assessing situations, not only about the game but also about individual players and their well-being. Learn the signs of fatigue!

Remember, as a coach you decide who plays, and ultimately your players participate in sports to play. If losing playing privileges does not motivate a player to follow the rules, then he or she is not motivated to play sports and probably does not belong on the team in the first place. It is perfectly normal that some children do not want to play sports. If this is the case you have to make an honest assessment and find out the child's motivation for playing. Is the child playing because of peer pressure or parental pressure? Perhaps you need to arrange a meeting with the parents to better assess the situation. If you find out that a player does not want to play it is best to address the situation immediately. This situation highlights another reason why the yelling model is dangerous. If players fear the coach, do you think a player who does not want to be there is going to talk to him or her? If you show players that you are able to address situations calmly, they will be more likely to open up to you. However, for the most part your players yearn to be out there and play in games. By establishing the precedent that players who do not follow the rules will lose playing privileges and then sticking to this rule, you can handle almost every situation.

Of course, taking away playing privileges can sometimes be a hard pill to swallow, particularly when it involves your best players. Coaches who are motivated solely by winning find this almost impossible to do and rely upon yelling and intimidation to discipline their team. There is no doubt that Vince Lombardi's speeches about winning at all costs are stirring. It is hard not to get caught up in this mentality. One important distinction is that Vince Lombardi was a coach for a professional football team. However, this point is often lost as youth coaches storm the playing fields fresh from watching YouTube videos of Lombardi's greatest speeches. As a youth coach you are coaching young people who will likely never play professionally. As an ethical youth coach you have the responsibility to treat every player equally. Just because one player is outstanding does not mean he or she cannot sit out for a game. Recall the slogan of The Center for Ethical Youth Coaching: "Winning is Something, but not Everything." Yes, we all love to win. However, this cannot be done at the cost of betraying our ethical duties as youth coaches.

The CEYC never advocates the use of profanity by a coach. Profanity creates a negative environment, which in turn fosters poor sportsmanship. Some coaches will defend their use of profanity as a way to motivate their team or stop a team from engaging in unruly behavior. However, research conducted by the International Sports Professional Association found that coaches use profanity more to motivate themselves than their players. When a coach swears he or she is using the swear word as an emotional trigger, one which acts to impassion their speech. Thus it is not really the swear word that players respond to but rather the heightened emotional state of the coach. So the next time you are tempted to swear, stop and talk in a firm and controlled manner and you will get the attention of your players.

It is important to be creative in your quest to motivate your team. Think more Gene Hackman from *Hoosiers* than Al Pacino from *Any Given Sunday*. A coach who has to use yelling and swearing to motivate his or her team is missing out on a great opportunity to truly motivate their players and not simply intimidate. Have fun with your effort to motivate your team. One of the great pleasures of youth coaching is leading a group of young athletes who are truly motivated. Remember, always keep your motivation positive, and focused on building up your team rather than breaking down the other team.

Another important distinction to make is between yelling and raising your voice on the sideline to be heard. Oftentimes a coach must raise his or her voice to be heard by the players on the field. The intention is of course not to yell at the team but rather to be heard by the players. However, to the causal onlooker it may appear that you are yelling at your team. There is not really much you can do in this situation, though if someone voices concern you can explain to him or her that you must raise your voice to be heard by the team. Make sure that when you call out plays or directions your voice is loud and in control. This will also indicate to people that you are seeking to be heard, not yelling.

Keywords:
Yelling
Cheering
Assessing the Situation

Questions:
1) Why is yelling not an acceptable form of communication in youth sports?
2) Why do some people feel that a coach is not doing their job unless they are yelling?
3) Describe the differences between "yelling" and "Cheering."

4) How can a coach handle an unruly player without yelling?
5) (True or False) It is okay to swear sometimes.
6) How can you minimize the chance of raising your voice to be heard from being interpreted as yelling?

Activities:

1) Create your own *Hoosiers*-type motivational speech.

Chapter 12
Self-Esteem and the Confidence Factor

One concept you may hear thrown around a lot is self-esteem. **Self-esteem**, simply put, is an individual's own assessment of their worth. Many factors go into determining an individual's self-esteem. It can be a complex process. An individual who suffers from extreme low self-esteem issues would be best served by seeing a licensed professional therapist, who is best equipped to deal with such issues. As a coach you will deal with players who have varying degrees of self-esteem, and it is important to protect the self-esteem of them all. Following the principles set forth in this book will ensure that you are doing everything in your power to preserve your players' self-esteem. In fact, you will be continually adding to it. If you observe a player with what appear to be self-esteem issues, it is important to not rush to conclusions. A well-intentioned coach who immediately sets up a meeting with a player's parents after determining that the player has low self-esteem can be asking for disaster if the player does not really have a problem. Imagine if a coach sat you down and told you that your child needed counseling because he or she has self-esteem issues. If the child has no real problems the meeting could get hostile. Remember, children have varying levels of self-esteem, and just because a player exhibits signs of low levels during your time with them does not mean that he or she has a problem. The same child may be supremely confident on the guitar. Please see Chapter 13, "Special Situations and First Aid," for more information on when and how to intervene in situations that may require extra attention.

Placing sole emphasis on boosting players' self-esteem may not be the most prudent coaching philosophy because of all the complexities and unknown variables involved. This does not mean a coach should shy away from opportunities to boost a player's self esteem; it means that a well-intentioned coach should not base all of his or her actions on the premise that they are boosting their players' self-esteem.

Let's restate the above: The Center for Ethical Youth Coaching is not implying that building players' self-esteem is not important, but it does advocate that self-esteem should not be the central theme of player development. Self-esteem is a complex overall appraisal of an individual's worth to him- or herself, and it is something that is hard for a coach to tackle in the limited interactions he or she has with players. Furthermore, most coaches are not trained to deal with self-esteem issues. Many of the techniques outlined in this book will already boost young athletes' self-esteem, because the principles promoted by the Ethical Youth Coach make up part of an individual's determination of their self-esteem. As an EYC coach it is your duty to be sensitive to players' self-esteem.

This highlights an important principle: a coach should focus on things that are within his or her **sphere of influence**. With so many variables that determine self-esteem a coach cannot conclusively determine how they are impacting players' self-esteem levels. A coach's sphere of influence is something that he or she can have a direct impact on and then observe this impact directly. For example, confidence is something that a coach can have a direct impact on and observe. The following is an example of a coach's impact on a player's confidence.

> *Jimmy is on his grade school basketball team and has difficulty with free throw shots. Whenever Jimmy goes to the line he loses confidence in his ability to shoot free throws, even though in practice he is the best free throw shooter on the team. One day after practice Jimmy's coach sits down with him and explains to him that there is no difference between shooting free throws during a game and shooting free throws in practice. The coach tells Jimmy that he must block out all the distractions and focus on the basket. The basket is the same height and he is the same distance away from it as in practice. He also reminds Jimmy that he is the best free throw shooters on the team. During the next game Jimmy makes eighty percent of his free throws, a*

significant improvement from previous games. With each free throw attempt the coach observes Jimmy's confidence grow. No longer does he approach the line timidly; he now walks to the line confidently and bounces the ball with authority.

The above is a perfect example of something that is in a coach's sphere of influence. Jimmy's coach saw a situation that he could impact and acted. The coach was then able to observe how his coaching affected Jimmy. The confidence boost that Jimmy's coach imparted to him is one of the most important things a coach can give a player. Confidence, unlike self-esteem, is something that is readily observable. Every coach should strive to build the confidence of his or her players.

One of the greatest ways you can preserve player self-esteem is by understanding **player diversity**. As a coach you will encounter players from different ethnicities, social backgrounds, socioeconomic statuses and religious backgrounds. An EYC coach never makes comments that can be perceived as culturally insensitive. Recognizing and embracing the diversity on your team is an important step toward being an EYC coach. However, if players or their parents do not "bring up" their culture or religious affiliation it is not appropriate to ask the players or their parents unless they make it clear that it is okay. The most important thing to keep in mind when dealing with your team is to be sensitive to racial issues and always err on the side of caution. Just because ninety percent of your team finds a cultural joke funny does not mean it is okay. And never assume a player's background, culture or religious affiliation simply because they "look a certain way."

By following the advice in this chapter you will help preserve player self-esteem and build confidence.

Keywords:
Self-Esteem
Sphere of Influence
Player Diversity

Questions:

1) How can you ensure that you are preserving a player's self-esteem?

2) (True or False) As soon as you observe a player with signs of low self-esteem you should set up a meeting with the player's parents.

3) (True or False) A child who has low levels of self-esteem in sports has low levels of self-esteem in all areas of his or her life.

4) Why is it not the best strategy to place all of your emphasis on building self-esteem?

5) (True or False) Confidence is within a coach's sphere of influence.

6) (True or False) It is always appropriate to ask a player their race and religion.

Chapter 13
Special Situations in Youth Coaching

Section Author: Dr. John Mayer

In this section we will discuss several real world situations that coaches may face. Discussion of these issues is not meant to be an exhaustive analysis but a condensed version of all the most important tools you will need. Review this chapter before each season. We strongly urge you to review the section on first aid several times throughout your season and to practice the techniques outlined therein.

Bullying and Teasing

The last decade has seen more and more research on the problem of **bullying and teasing**. It is encouraging to see so much attention paid to this traditionally neglected area of aggressive social behavior. The findings are disturbing. One of the most recent studies (2008) and one of the few longitudinal studies highlight an alarming number of adolescents who bully – 58.4%. The US Secret Service reported in 2002 that two-thirds of all perpetrators of youth violent crimes were teased or bullied prior to the event. The National Threat Assessment Center found that attackers in more than 66% of the thirty-seven mass school shootings were persecuted or bullied by others and that revenge was the overriding motive.

Further, studies are showing that bullies who are not corrected of this behavior are very likely to develop psychiatric and psychological problems in early adulthood. And the victims of bullying display a greater risk of psychosocial maladjustment as well as somatic complaints (e.g. headaches, sleep problems, stomach aches) than other young people.

Bullying and teasing among young people is a very serious problem.

The most common tactics of bullies are:

1) Belittling the other child on how they look physically or how they speak. This constitutes 61% of all bullying behavior.
2) Creating rumors about someone. 60% of all bullying behavior.
3) Hitting, pushing, and/or slapping another child. 56% of all bullying behavior.
4) Making a sexual comment or gesture toward another. 52% of all bullying behavior.
5) Belittling another child about his or her religion or race. 26% of all bullying behavior.

      Fact: Boys tend to be bullied physically.
      Fact: Girls tend to be bullied emotionally.

A remarkable fact about the above statistics is how difficult it is for the victim to defend themselves against the most common form of bullying, i.e., how we look or how we talk. We cannot instantly change these things, yet bullies target them most commonly in their attacks on others. Also, as we grow up our physical looks are changing all the time. At times in our development we may have looked awkward, maybe even different from other children. Some of us grew faster and some slower than the majority of our peers. Thus, these attacks on one's looks and speech are particularly cruel. Yet in the large scope of things, who can tell what the perfect ears look like? The perfect smile, the perfect hair color or style, or the perfect nose – do any of these really exist? No, they don't.

This suggests a good way to help victims of bullies and teasers. Tell them to look around, and ask them those questions. Who is perfect? Explain to them that your looks are unique to you and they help define who you are. Your looks are nothing to be ashamed about.

Most bullying and teasing takes place in schools and school-sponsored activities such as sports.

This is not because schools and sports create bullies and teasers. When it comes to school it is because school is the time and place in a child's life in which they spend the most concentrated time together with other children. The fact that children spend such long periods of time with other children under one roof is the biggest reason why these behaviors occur more in school than anywhere else. Another reason why schools have so many instances of teasing and bullying is that school is not only a place of academic learning, but also a place of social learning. Children experiment during school time with styles of behaving toward each other. By definition, "experiment" means that some behaviors will not work or they may be negative. In addition to all the above conditions shared with schools, sports is in a unique position in that most athletes participate because *they want to*. Playing sports is highly valued in the life of the young person, and the value placed on it "ups the ante" on social and emotional attachment.

School and Sports are not to blame for bullying and teasing.

Most often bullying is <u>not</u> an impulsive act; rather it is something that has been brewing inside the bully for some time. This is important to know because it indicates that we should not dismiss the act of bullying as something temporary, a mindless action of a child's immature or unsocialized mind, or even a phase that will go away by itself. We know that bullying is none of these.

Bullies show bullying tendencies well before they take action. For example, we now know that bullies have high levels of moral disengagement. That is, they show behaviors, thoughts or kinds of language that are mean, cruel and/or manipulative. Bullies show high degrees of aggression early on in their life. They also typically come from families that monitor them less. And they are more susceptible to peer pressure, seeking approval and status from their peers rather than from their parents or other adults.

Bullying and teasing behavior is not normal for children and we have to stop believing that it is acceptable. The bully has an emotional, psychological and/or social deficit at this time in their life. I emphasize, "at this time in their life." Psychologists have seen that many children who engage in bullying do not grow up to have these deficits later in their lives, and many grow up to be anything but bullies. However, make no mistake, bullies whose actions go uncorrected will tend to develop psychological disorders of serious magnitude.

It is a fact that bullies are less mature than other children. "Less mature" may seem to be a casual term, but for the professional it means that these children are developmentally delayed. This is a disorder and not to be taken lightly.

Bullying doesn't appear out of the blue.

The aim of bullying behavior is varied, but the fact is that bullying behavior exists and continues because it <u>works</u> for the bully. It enables the bully to get what he or she wants out of the other child or peer group (see the bulleted list below). It is important to accept this fact. We will not eradicate the behavior by denying how well it works for some children. When a coach supports bullying behavior by dismissing it as just being aggressive as a player or because it comes from a star player, this gives the wrong impression to everyone on the team. And it will inevitably come back to hurt the coach in some way.

Bullying continues because it works for the bully. We have to stop it from working.

So, what are the common aims of a child in being a bully? Here are the top goals of this behavior:

- Obtaining power over another or in the social group. It can give the bully a false sense of leadership or status in the peer group.
- Getting attention from others.
- Insecurity.
- Discharge of rage.
- Discharge of anger.
- Trying to cope with family problems by taking negative feelings out on others.
- General release from emotional problems such as depression, anxiety, sadness, etc.

- Modeling a social style engaged in by parents or other family members.
- Trying to fit in with a gang.
- Gang "wannabe" behavior, i.e., copying behaviors they perceive as those of gang members, thugs, or those in the media who have a "gangster," thug, or criminal persona.
- Trying to be dominant in the social life of a school.
- Modeling or being taught this behavior by non-family members such as coaches, tutors, scout leaders, etc.

Bullying and teasing can be eliminated. Chances of young people following the right path are increased when all the environments that children travel through are leading them in the right direction. Coaches can have a positive impact on helping prevent bullying.

All the environments that a child travels through should respond similarly to bullying and teasing.

Here are specific actions that adults in children's environments need to take to eliminate bullying and teasing.

- Discipline children who are bullying and teasing others when you observe it happening.
- Do not make light of the actions of bullies and teasers.
- Do not allow, and therefore discipline, even slight behaviors that are in the direction of teasing or bullying, such as name-calling, hitting, disrespect, taunting, and put-downs.
- Treat bullying behavior as seriously as any other violation of rules.
- There is nothing wrong with imposing consequences when you <u>suspect that</u> bullying has happened.
- Increase the supervision of the perpetrators.
- Always model appropriate behavior yourself. Do not tease or put down others, particularly those younger than you, in order to be humorous, teach a lesson, be motivational, get them to behave correctly, etc. Teasing, sarcasm, prodding, nagging and yelling are all behaviors in adults that have been proven time and again not to work.

- Be a cooperative team player with other adults when in a children's environment. As a parent don't negate what your spouse says to the children in front of them. Pick an appropriate time to share differences in discipline, rule setting, privileges, etc.
- Counsel the bully or teaser. Show them appropriate ways to get the same goals accomplished. There is nothing wrong with being popular, funny, or even having power, but it is wrong to achieve it at the expense of others. The focus of your counseling of the bully should be on what needs are being met by this behavior. Counsel the bully with compassion, not blame. This approach doesn't take away the consequences of their actions. Try to understand why they approach social situations with bullying and teasing. When appropriate, help them understand things that may be confusing to them and that they therefore tease others about. Some examples of this are making fun of someone's eyeglasses or braces, the way a disabled person walks, a speech impediment, etc. Help them to understand that when they bully someone, something has gone wrong inside them. Try and uncover what has damaged them. Make sure you emphasize that you care about them and will try to help them, just like you would help anyone who has something go wrong inside them.
- Make sure you don't let bullying or teasing work for those who do this.

The above actions focus on the bully or teaser. There are also actions you can take to help the victims of bullying or teasing:

- Make sure the victim understands that it is the bully who is wrong. This is very important and sounds simple to do. Emphasize to the victim that they are Ok and that it is the bully/teaser who is damaged at this time in their life. Many victims of teasing and bullying begin to doubt who they are, that they are Ok or that something about them is not like the other children.

- Don't assume that children know how to solve their problems. In fact, all of this is new to them and they need specific advice on how to solve social conflicts.
- Tell them your story. Let them know that they are not alone and that you were teased and maybe picked on as a child. Most of us were, at some time or another. Share how you handled the situation. Or, if you didn't handle it in an appropriate way, what you learned and how you now know how to handle it better. Be honest. Kids have the best lie-dar of anyone.
- Always encourage children to report incidents of being teased or bullied.
- If a peer group is hard on your players, understand that this is inevitably going to happen and sometimes our best efforts cannot stop it. Often in this case the best thing we can do is encourage and provide opportunities for kids to develop friendships that are more likely to lead to positive friendships apart from the negative peer group. This is where such opportunities as social clubs, <u>sports teams</u>, arts activities, scouting, etc., come into play and are extremely valuable. For this reason, coaches can play a critical role in stopping bullying.
- Increase supervision of the victim; protect the victim from the bully. Be around them more. Possibly in an unobtrusive way, but be more of a presence in the child's life.
- Build the victim's self-confidence. Praise them for their courage in speaking up about the teasing and bullying.
- Make sure they feel successful in activities they enjoy. Praise and honor them at every opportunity, though also be genuine and honest in this effort.
- Help to create a rich, full life for them, so that if another child is a problem it doesn't become their whole world. Bullying and teasing hurts worse when the relationship with the perpetrator is the most important one to the young person/victim.

Drawing on all the research we have accumulated on this subject, we've found that there are three "power tools" children themselves can use to help eliminate bullying and teasing. This is how we change the "peer environment" discussed in the last section. Little else works as well as these techniques.

POWER TOOLS TO STOP BULLYING AND TEASING:
1) **IGNORE** the bully and ignore the teasing.
2) **DON'T REACT** in any way to the actions of the bully or teaser.
3) **REPORT** any bullying or teasing to the adult(s) in charge and to your parents, always.

All of these are hard for children to do. It is hard to ignore someone who is hurting your feelings. The child may be in classes with the perpetrator, or sports or after-school activities. Here is where you as a coach and the parents, teachers, or tutors may have to step in to physically ensure that a victim is not in the presence of a bully. The important point here is to instruct young people to stay away from the bully or teaser. This takes away the reinforcement or reward that the bully/teaser obtains from their actions.

Even when a child can ignore the bully or teaser, the second power tool is even more difficult for young people to accomplish. It may seem to be the same as the first power tool, but it has important differences. Ignoring the bully or teaser is one thing; not reacting in any way to the bully is another. Not reacting means not flinching, not rolling your eyes, not changing your direction, not ceasing to raise your hand in class, not stopping getting great grades, and most of all, not returning the negative behavior with another negative behavior. That means not shoving back, hitting them harder, calling them a better name, etc.

In the past, many parents and other authority figures would try to handle the bullying situation using these latter negative methods. "Well, you go back there and punch him in the nose harder and that will end it." Or, "Hmmmm....let me help you think about what you can say to them tomorrow that will hurt their feelings right back."

These techniques simply don't work for the vast majority of

bullying and teasing situations. They don't work because of what I call the "Fastest Gun in the West" phenomenon. This means that if you use these strong-arm techniques you are going to eventually encounter someone who is stronger or who has a more acid tongue. In both cases, the child will get hurt, possibly very seriously, and the bullying hasn't ended. These are similar to the conditions that existed in the cold war. We learned in that conflict that the end result of hostilities would be the annihilation of the human race, not the end of the threats. Stop teaching your children to do this.

The Fight Fire with Fire and Cold War tactics that try to stop bullying and teasing simply don't work!

Finally, the last power tool is to tell an adult. Many children are taught incorrectly that telling on someone is bad. You're a tattletale, a snitch, a narc, etc. But, remember, there is something wrong with the bully. Shouldn't we be teaching our children to help others in need? This scenario is no different from that of a fellow player being physically sick. Shouldn't we be teaching our children to come to their aid? Let the teacher know. Let the coach know. This is good moral behavior. Create an atmosphere on your team where it is good to help one another.

Drug and Alcohol Use

Players of all ages confront the reality of **drug** and **alcohol** use that surrounds them in this society. For underage players, alcohol is an illegal substance. In the remainder of this section we will discuss alcohol and other illegal drugs with one term, *substance abuse*. You should make no mistake that alcohol is just as deadly a problem as any illegal drug. In fact, statistics on illness consistently show that *the abuse of alcohol is by far the #1 drug problem in the United States*. Do not diminish the dangerousness of alcohol use and abuse.

The scope of this manual is not to go in depth on the social issues surrounding substance abuse and rally coaches around prevention and intervention, but rather to arm the coach with the tools to recognize when substance abuse may be affecting a player or a team, and therefore putting that player and the other players in danger.

Substance abuse, particularly alcohol abuse, is well ingrained in the culture of sports. Because of this, substance abuse is a surprisingly neglected special situation in coaching. Youth sports are replete with stories of horrible modeling of substance abuse by coaches. Start a discussion with any parent of an athlete and you are sure to hear about the coach who blew smoke in the faces of the players during a practice huddle, players given beer after a big victory, celebration parties with underage drinking, steroid use, pain killers, anti-inflammatories, alcohol use fundraisers and on and on. Ethical coaches have a responsibility to *MODEL* appropriate behavior regarding such substances and to surround their team with an atmosphere that advocates a positive lifestyle. Promoting drinking or any illegal substance use is wrong and quite frankly will rip your team apart.

An example may be most helpful to illustrate how disastrous it can be if a coach neglects their ethical duty to model appropriate behavior toward substance abuse. A powerhouse high school football program was headed into a season they had been waiting for since this group of boys were freshmen. It was arguably the most talented group of athletes this school had ever had, and this was a school that had produced many state champions. Unfortunately, many of these boys came from an area around the school that was notorious for parents who allowed their children to drink openly as teenagers and turned a blind eye to marijuana use. The cultural mindset seemed to be, "We did our share of partying when we were teens." Or, "I'd rather they drink with me in my presence." By the time this talented group were juniors a culture of drinking and pot smoking was ingrained in a core group, including several team captains and the quarterback. Even though these players were not the majority of the team, their raucous ways modeled to the other players a standard of a lack of dedication. Several of the coaches knew about the partying ways of these boys, but dismissed it as a sign of their being tough kids who go full tilt at everything they do. Predictably, this group's junior and senior seasons were disappointments. The team didn't come close to a state championship. The coaches realized what a mistake they made in rationalizing the players' drinking and drug use. They vowed never to allow this type of culture to infect a team again.

In this example the coaches had the advantage of living in the same area as the boys did, so could observe them drinking and using drugs, though they did nothing to stop it. Often a coach doesn't have the luxury of seeing kids drink or use drugs, so how could one tell if a player is using a substance? The only sure way is to have the player do a drug test. People may boast to you that they can always tell if a young person is high on drugs. If one of your fellow coaches makes such a statement you should not rely on this assessment. It is dangerous to do so. No one is an expert on telling if a youth is on drugs just by looking at them. If they brag that they can, they are either a liar or have too big an ego or both. Even professionals in the substance abuse field will tell you that behavioral clues alone (how a player looks or acts) are not absolute verifications that a player is using substances. Behavioral clues should only put the question in your head that this player could be drinking or using drugs.

Keeping in mind that behavioral clues are speculative we will highlight several actions and behaviors that indicate the need to investigate whether the player is using substances:

- A sudden change in behavior from a consistent player.
- Dramatic ups and downs in behavior.
- Change in coordination and/or control of their body; clumsiness.
- Slurred speech.
- Poor vision.
- Dilated pupils.
- Red, bloodshot eyes.
- Shortness of breath—getting winded easily.
- Heart palpitations. (They may complain of chest pains or a racing heart rate.)
- Slowness in responding to instruction or following directives.
- Forgetfulness.
- Mood swings—although this is tough with teens, who have big hormonal shifts naturally.
- Sudden increase in body mass. (Steroid use.)
- Constant reddish skin. (Steroid use.)
- Very brittle, easily scratched/cut/bruised skin. (Steroid use.)

- Excessive sweating—not within the normal age range of your players. (Steroid use and other drugs as well.)
- Physical hyperactivity.
- Changes in motivation or commitment to the sport.

The best course of action to take as a coach of a young person who shows one or more of these signs is to address your concerns with the athlete. If this does not ease your suspicions the next step would be to discuss your concerns with the player's parent(s) and finally, if both of these steps do not satisfy your concerns, you should insist that the player get a medical permission note to release the player to participate. This release should include a complete drug test. Seem severe? We would do no less for other physical conditions that place the player and YOU in danger of something happening to that player while in your supervision. Don't take chances with substance abuse.

Finally, one of the most effective things you can do as a coach to prevent the possibility that you will need to confront a situation of substance abuse in a player is to MODEL appropriate drug-free behavior yourself. Watch how you hold yourself up to the players as an example. Don't make jokes or speak casually in ways that might make drinking and drugs seem desirable. Watch how you talk with your fellow coaches and other adults involved in your program. Do this even if you don't believe that the players are in earshot. Young people pick up such conversations like magic. Don't surround your players with visual messages about drinking or drug use. Do you have a beer or liquor ad on the fence of your field? What do you think this is going to convey? A key ingredient in preventing young people from getting involved in substances is stopping the inappropriate modeling they are surrounded by in our society. Have control over your players' environment.

Physical/Sexual Abuse

Coaches in many states are <u>not</u> mandated reporters of child abuse. But, if you are a teacher, chances are that you are indeed mandated by the state in which you work to report such abuse. If you coach young people we advise that you check your state's requirements on the mandated reporting of child abuse. Being a mandated reporter carries the legal obligation of reporting child abuse to the local branch of the relevant state agency if you suspect that a child has been abused. If you are an assistant coach on a team on which the head coach is a mandated reporter, and you suspect that one of your players is a victim of child abuse, we advise you to bring this to the attention of the head coach and discuss a report to the state authorities.

Using caution in reporting physical or sexual abuse of a player is strongly advised. Children and teenagers can perceive abuse differently from the legal definition. A call to the state authority may be inappropriate in a situation where a child has misperceived firm discipline. A hasty call may prompt the parents to confront you. Filing such a report can also create a worse situation for the child/ teenager. The state authority could find the report of suspected abuse to be unwarranted, and the child then possibly receiving stronger consequences than at first.

There are no simple answers to the issue of physical or sexual abuse. Each situation is most properly handled on a case-by-case basis. However, a few guidelines are helpful when you function as a coach in the lives of young people.

- Communicate your suspicions with your colleagues. Talk to other coaches and other adults involved in the player's life about what you have observed or been told. Don't be a "Lone Ranger."
- If a player tells you about being hit or beaten by a parent or adult ask them to show you any marks that were left on their body. But, use common sense here. If the marks are on an intimate part of their body do not try to observe this alone. Have a colleague of the same sex as the player with you, or better yet, refer this examination to a team/ school nurse or doctor, or the team trainer. The player may be eager to show you marks on personal parts of their body, but if you are alone have them stop until you can be with another adult.
- Collect information before you act on your suspicions. If you see bruises on a player in a locker room, obviously such marks could have a variety of sources from participation

in sports. Again, check with colleagues, teachers, and health professionals before confronting the player or their parents.

- The safety and well-being of the player is the most important consideration here. Do not keep abusive situations secret even if the player asks you not to speak up. If you suspect the player is in danger it is important to make a report to the authorities. The player's safety is more important than whether they will like you. Unlike a doctor, as a coach you are not protected or governed by laws on confidential relationships. The player may not like you for reporting abuse, but you may be saving their life.

- Unless the abuse is a result of some inappropriate team hazing or bullying, most of the time this is <u>not</u> a team issue. There is no reason to discuss the player's experience of abuse with the rest of the team. Such disclosure will just add to the player's emotional pain.

- Make sure the abuse victim receives medical attention.

- Make sure that the abuse victim receives mental health attention.

- Don't minimize the power you have as a coach in the life of this young person; you have the authority to help guide the player and their parents as to corrective steps in this situation. Sports are typically voluntary. The player and their parents often strongly desire for the player to be on the team. The coach has a status that many other adults in kids' lives don't enjoy. They may listen to you more than any other adult in authority. Don't dismiss your role in a potential abuse situation by such casual statements as, "I'm only their coach – what can I do."

- You may not be legally obligated to report abuse, but think of your moral obligation to protect the player.

Physical Contact/ Touching

Always be careful when engaging in physical contact or touching with players. Even inappropriate accidental touching can expose a coach to liability. Let's look at the following example:

Coach Jim carelessly walks behind a female basketball player to help her with free throws. While helping her, his groin accidentally comes into contact with the player's buttocks.

While this contact was an accident, the main concern is that coach Jim "carelessly" walked behind the player. Coach Jim gave no thought to the fact that he has entered his player's personal space. Furthermore, while, in his players, personal space inappropriate contact was made that could have been avoided if coach Jim executed care while assisting the player. What if the player became upset by this contact? What if she had been a victim of abuse or inappropriate touching in the past? The above coach is entering into an area of vulnerability and certainly potential liability. Attorneys often caution people that these are "grey" areas of behavior and your actions put you at risk for lawsuits. The bottom line is you should always be mindful of the physical contact you have with your players. The above is not meant to scare you from contact with your players, as contact is often a necessary part of coaching; it is meant to make you mindful of properly executing this contact and not being careless.

Safety and First Aid

Compiling a Well-Furnished Coach's First Aid Kit

There are several items that should be in a First Aid Kit to ensure your ability to respond to a variety of situations. It is important that you check and restock your First Aid Kit frequently – once a month or after each use of the supplies in the kit – to ensure that necessary materials are always available. It is often beneficial to create a checklist of the items needed in the kit as well the minimum quantity that you should have of each item. Print out this list and keep it in or near the First Aid Kit. It is also important that all coaches are aware of the location of the First Aid Kit to ensure ease of access to the supplies. The following should be in the First Aid Kit at all times:

- Adhesive tape (one or two rolls)
- Aluminum finger splint (one or two)
- Antibiotic ointment, i.e. Neosporin (one tube)
- Antiseptic pads (10)
- Bandages (Ace wraps, Band-aids) in a variety of sizes
- Instant cold packs (one or two)
- Cotton balls or cotton-tipped swabs (10 or more)
- Disposable gloves (two pairs each of small, medium, and large)
- Gauze pads (three or four) and roller gauze (one roll)
- Plastic bags for disposal of contaminated items (two or three)
- Hydrogen peroxide (one bottle)
- Scissors (one or two pairs) and tweezers (one)
- Thermometer (one) with disposable sleeves (one box)
- Barrier device for CPR (one each for infant, child, and adult)
- Sterile eye wash, i.e. saline solution (one bottle)
- Eye goggles (one or two)
- First Aid manual
- Instant hand sanitizer (one or two bottles)
- Flashlight (one) and extra batteries (one or two boxes)
- Emergency contact information (local emergency services, poison control)

Medications
- Tylenol
- Aspirin for chest pain (___never___ give to children under the age of 12)
- Antihistamines (Benadryl)
- Calamine lotion

Note: This is a general list of supplies that should ensure effective response to a variety of situations. Additional supplies may be necessary depending on the sport and the age/sex of the players.

It is also beneficial to have players list all their allergies, whether environmental or drug allergies. This list should be kept in the first aid kit itself and in the team files.

When to Dial 9-1-1

Whenever you are uncertain about how to respond to a situation in which an individual's health and safety is compromised, call 9-1-1. However, **NEVER** leave a victim alone. Easy access to a means of communication should be available in all areas while you coach. When someone is with you, instruct him or her to dial 9-1-1 immediately. If you are alone, in a situation involving an adult or young adult, dial 9-1-1 before beginning CPR (discussed below) OR, with a child, perform one minute of CPR and then dial 9-1-1.

When calling 9-1-1 or local emergency services, provide the operator with the following information:

- Location
- A number where you can be reached
- Details on the type of emergency
- The person's current condition and/or the condition in which you found him or her

Remember! It is crucial that you have emergency contact information readily available and displayed wherever you are coaching and the players are practicing or playing in a game.

First Aid for Choking Victims (Adult or Child)

In ANY situation in which someone's health or safety is compromised the first step is ALWAYS to assess the situation.

Assess whether the victim can cough or talk by asking, "Are you choking?" If the victim signals yes, either by shaking their head yes or clutching their hand to their throat (which is the universal sign for choking), perform the Heimlich maneuver (discussed next) until the object is expelled.

Other signs that indicate choking include:

- Difficulty breathing or gasping for air
- Inability to talk or cough
- Loss of consciousness or cyanotic skin (bluish coloration that typically occurs as a late sign of impaired oxygenation)

The Heimlich maneuver

First, position yourself behind the victim. Perform five back blows to determine if the object can be expelled that way. Using the palm of your hand, firmly strike between the victim's shoulder blades a maximum of five (5) times. This may be enough to dislodge the object. If this is not effective, create a fist with your dominant hand and wrap it around the victim's torso just above the naval. Take your non-dominant hand and wrap it around the fist. Position your hands slightly above the victim's navel and just below their rib cage. Have them lean forward slightly, or if the victim is not able to follow commands, push the torso forward slightly. With your fist, press firmly into the abdomen with quick, upward thrusts. It is crucial that you determine that they are choking before performing the Heimlich maneuver, as it can be detrimental to internal organs. Perform five abdominal thrusts. If the object is not expelled from the victim's airway repeat these steps until the object is expelled or the victim becomes unresponsive. If the victim becomes unresponsive, lower him or her to the ground away from danger and call 9-1-1 and begin CPR. Exception: if the victim is a child perform one minute of CPR and then call 9-1-1. **NEVER** leave the victim alone!

If the victim is **pregnant** or **obese**, a chest thrust may be substituted for the abdominal thrust. First, as with any emergency situation, assess if they are choking (as discussed above). Then, perform five back blows to attempt to dislodge the object. If unsuccessful, wrap you arms around the victim's chest and place one hand just below the breastbone and above the lowest rib. Perform the same steps as discussed above. You may need to have the victim sit down if they are taller than you and proper placement of your hands is unattainable. Perform the chest thrust five times. If the object does not dislodge, repeat the steps. If the victim becomes unresponsive, call 9-1-1 and begin CPR.

Abdominal thrusts may cause complications such as damage to internal organs. A victim who has received abdominal thrusts should be examined immediately by a healthcare provider to ensure that life-threatening complications do not arise.

The Basics of Cardiopulmonary Resuscitation (CPR)

How you respond to an emergency situation is determined by your training and comfort level. Remember, doing something is **ALWAYS** better then not doing anything, even if your knowledge and skills are not 100%.

Time is Critical!

For an unconscious person who is not breathing, it takes very few minutes for brain damage to occur and approximately eight to ten minutes before death can occur.

Components of CPR

    1) Chest Compressions
    2) Mouth-to-mouth rescue breathing

The very first step in any emergency is to ASSESS the situation. First, assess the scene in which you find the victim to ensure safety for yourself and the victim. If you foresee danger to yourself or the victim, move yourself and the victim to safety immediately! If the victim is unconscious, firmly pat the bottom of the victim's foot or shake him or her and loudly ask, "Are you OK?" Exception: If you suspect a neck or spinal cord injury do NOT move or shake the victim unless you and the victim are in immediate danger. If the victim does not respond and other people are nearby, have someone call for emergency assistance immediately and initiate CPR.

When performing CPR, remember **ABC**.

- <u>A</u>irway
- <u>B</u>reathing
- <u>C</u>irculation

Airway

Carefully position the victim on their back on a firm surface and kneel next to the victim's shoulders on the side where your dominant hand is facing the victim's head and your non-dominant hand is facing his or her torso. Open the victim's airway using the head-tilt and chin-lift. To perform the head-tilt and chin-lift complete the following steps:

- Tilt the victim's head back and place the palm of your hand on his or her forehead.
- With the other hand, gently lift the chin forward to assist in opening the airway.

Exception: If a neck or spinal cord injury is suspected, do not tilt the head back. Instead, position yourself behind the victim's head and place your hands on both sides of the victim's jaw. Gently push the jaw forward to open the airway.

- Look inside the victim's mouth for the presence of a foreign object. If present, do not attempt to remove the object as this may cause the object to become pushed further into the airway. Instead, perform chest compressions (soon to be discussed) until the object is expelled.

If you believe that the victim is unconscious due to a heart attack, skip the rescue breaths (discussed under Breathing) and begin chest compressions (discussed under Circulation).

Breathing

Next, look, listen, and feel to assess for normal breathing. Do this by performing the following steps:

- With the victim's head still tilted back, place your ear

over the victim's mouth and <u>look</u> for the rise and fall of the victim's chest.

- Simultaneously, <u>listen</u> for breath sounds from his or her nose or mouth and <u>feel</u> for the victim's breath on your cheek.
- Do not take more than five to ten seconds to complete this step.
- Note: If any of these are present, call for help and do not initiate CPR.

If breathing is not felt, give one rescue breath by following the steps below and look, listen, and feel for normal breathing.

To give rescue breaths, first pinch the victim's nose closed with your thumb and index finger, with your other hand still on the victim's forehead. If a barrier device (usually a plastic covering) is available, cover the victim's mouth with the barrier device and secure the device with one hand to create a seal. If there is not a barrier device available, cover the victim's mouth with your mouth and give one rescue breath.

To create an airtight seal:

- Place the barrier device over the victim's mouth using the bridge of the nose as a landmark. Make sure the victim's head remains tilted back to maintain an open airway.
- Once the barrier device is positioned over the victim's nose and mouth, create a "C" shape with your thumb and index finger on your dominant hand. Place your index finger on the border of the mask on the side of the nose opposite to the side you are on, and your thumb on the border of the mask on the side of the nose closest to you. Use your non-dominant thumb and index finger to pinch the border of the barrier device against the chin. Press firmly against the mask.

Give a rescue breath of one second duration and watch for the rise and fall of the chest to determine if the breath was effective. If the chest does not rise, perform the head-tilt, chin-lift maneuver again to re-establish an open airway and repeat the steps above.

Circulation

Assess the carotid pulse (just below the victim's jaw on the neck) with two fingers for five to ten seconds. Recheck every two seconds during the delivery of CPR. If no pulse is felt or cyanosis (bluish color of lips) is present, begin chest compressions. To perform chest compressions:

- Place the palm of the dominant hand over the victim's chest between over the victim's chest at the sternum, between the nipples. Place the non-dominant hand over the hand positioned on the victim's chest. Intertwine your fingers and keep your elbows straight, with your shoulders directly above your hands.
- Push straight down using your upper body weight, pushing hard and fast. Push down 1½ to 2 times the width of the victim's chest for an adult and 1/3 to ½ times the width of the victim's chest for a child or infant. Perform compressions at a rate of 100 compressions a minute. This is very quick and it is beneficial to count out loud as you are performing compressions. *Take a minute now to determine this rate by timing yourself for one minute and counting to 100. This well help you ascertain if you need to adjust the rate.*
- After delivery of 30 compressions, give two rescue breaths and return to compressions.
- One cycle of CPR is classified as a 30 compressions to two rescue breaths (30:2) ratio. Perform five cycles of CPR. If someone is with you, designate one person to give rescue breaths and the other person to perform chest compressions.
- If after five cycles of CPR the victim has not regained consciousness, continue to perform CPR until the

The Principles of Ethical Youth Coaching

emergency medical team arrives or you are no longer physically able to effectively perform CPR.

- If you are with another person, switch between giving rescue breaths and performing chest compressions. CPR is an extremely arduous task! It is very important to conserve energy by alternating the roles of giving rescue breaths and chest compressions.

- If the victim has not regained consciousness after five cycles of CPR, attach an Automated External Defibrillator (AED), if available, and deliver a rescue shock if advised by the device (discussed below).

Automated External Defibrillator (AED)

Every school should have an AED in a designated area known to all employees. In addition, it should be noticeably marked and placed in an area that can be easily accessed. AED provides an individual with detailed instructions on how to operate the device. If you are uncomfortable using an AED, a 9-1-1 operator can instruct you on the appropriate steps to operate the device.

Take the pads that are provided in the AED and attach them to the victim. Remove the paper protector on the pads (there is an adhesive side which should be placed on the victim and a non-adhesive side to attach the wires). Most AEDs have diagrams to demonstrate proper placement of the pads. Place one pad below the left nipple, and the other pad above the right nipple. If the victim has a hairy chest, attach the sticky side of the AED pad to the victim's chest and quickly remove it. Then place a new pad on the chest in the designated locations. Most AEDs will have at least two sets of pads. It is important to routinely check the AED device to ensure that proper equipment is available for an emergency situation.

When using an AED on a child (one to eight years of age), use pediatric pads, if available. Place one pad on the middle of the child's chest, between the nipples. Place the second pad on the child's back, between the shoulder blades. NEVER use an AED on an infant (younger than one year of age).

After the pads are attached, continue to follow the AED's prompts. It will instruct you to press "analyze" and avoid touching the victim.

The AED will analyze the victim's heart rate and determine if a shock is advised. If advised, loudly announce "Everyone clear?" Press the shock button once you have determined that no one is touching the victim. After the shock is administered, the AED will prompt you to deliver another shock or begin CPR. *Each AED will provide you with prompts on how to effectively deliver a rescue shock.*

CPR on a Child (one year of age to puberty)
The steps for performing CPR are the same on a child as on an adult. However, there are a few differences that you should understand.

- If you are alone, perform five cycles of CPR (approximately one minute duration if the rate of compressions is 100/min) before calling 9-1-1 or using an AED.
- For chest compressions, use the palm of ONE hand and only press down 1/3 to ½ the width of the child's chest.
- Provide more gentle rescue breaths than you would with an adult. If you give rescue breaths to a child as you would for an adult, you may hyperventilate the child, which can cause concurrent lung tissue damage.
- If two rescuers are available, provide 15 compressions for every two breaths. If you are alone, provide 30 chest compressions for every two breaths, as you would for an adult.

Critical Points to Remember for CPR
Quality CPR improves the victim's chance of survival. The following are critical points to understand:

- Push hard and fast at a speed equivalent to 100 compressions per minute. It is beneficial to time yourself while practicing compressions to familiarize yourself with the correct rate.
- Allow the chest to fully recoil between each compression.
- Minimize interruptions while providing chest

compressions. Interruptions should be kept to less than 10 seconds.

- Avoid hyperventilation, especially with a child or infant.

What to do in Specific Emergency and Non-Emergency Medical Situations

Emergency and non-emergency medical situations can arise at any time, in any place, and to someone of any age. In order to promptly and effectively respond, it is crucial that you understand and are able to identify the symptoms of conditions that compromise an individual's health and safety.

Heart Attack (Myocardial Infarction, MI)

Many tend to think of those who have suffered a heart attack as only older, overweight individuals who smoke and lead a sedentary lifestyle. However, that is not true. Yes, these factors do increase the risk of a heart attack, but it can happen to anyone. Individuals in their 20s who are active and healthy suffer heart attacks. These individuals may even be at a higher risk of death, as the appropriate life-saving measures may not be implemented in a timely manner. Therefore, to reduce the risk of death or life-long morbidity, it is important to identify the symptoms of a heart attack and provide a quick response.

If you notice any of the following symptoms, call 9-1-1 or local emergency services immediately:

- Chest pain or lasting discomfort that is unrelieved by rest or nitroglycerin. Chest discomfort is the most important sign of a heart attack, especially if it radiates to the left arm or jaw.
- Increased perspiration or shortness of breath accompanied by weakness or fatigue.
- Dizziness and fainting are likely to occur as well.

If there is aspirin readily available, take one or two tablets with a full glass of water (follow administration instructions on bottle), unless contraindicated due to a bleeding disorder or aspirin allergy. <u>Never give aspirin to a child.</u>

If you are with a victim who has become unconscious and you believe it is due to a heart attack, begin CPR immediately! Unless certified in CPR, skip the rescue breaths and immediately begin chest compressions.

Anaphylaxis (Allergic Reaction)

Anaphylaxis can occur within minutes and can last up to several hours after exposure to an allergy-causing substance. A wide range of substances can cause an anaphylactic reaction including:

- Insect venom
- Pollen
- Latex
- Certain drugs and food
- An unknown cause

Signs and symptoms of anaphylaxis include but are not limited to the following:

- Swelling
- Itching
- Hives or rash
- Difficulty breathing; gasping for air

If an anaphylactic reaction is suspected, immediately call 9-1-1 or local emergency medical services. Look for special medications that the victim may have with them to treat the attack, such as an inhaler or an EpiPen. Administer the drug as directed. If the individual has an EpiPen or inhaler they should usually be able to self-administer the medication. However, if you find the victim unconscious or they are incapable of administering it on their own, you must administer the drug. If you are uncomfortable or unfamiliar with administering epinephrine, stay on the line with the 9-1-1 operator to have them coach you through the administration. An EpiPen is usually administered by pressing an auto-injector located at the top of the pen, opposite to the end with the needle. Press the injector against a muscular area on the victim's body (such as the thigh or upper arm) and hold it in place for at least 10 seconds to ensure that all the medication is administered. After administering the injection, massage the injection site to increase the rate of absorption.

If the victim has an open airway, administer an antihistamine such as Benadryl, if available. Remember, only administer it if you are certain that the victim can swallow the medication without choking. Anaphylactic reactions commonly cause the airway to swell, making swallowing a pill impossible.

Loosen the victim's clothing and have them lay in the Trendelenburg position (on their back with their head lower than their feet). If vomiting occurs, have the victim lay on their side to prevent choking.

If the victim becomes unconscious, breathless, has no pulse, or signs of cyanosis are observed, initiate CPR.

Seizures

In the event of a seizure there are a few important do's and don'ts to consider.

DO:

- Free the victim from potential hazardous objects
- Turn the victim to their side if possible, otherwise position them flat on their back, free from danger
- STAY WITH THE VICTIM AT ALL TIMES
- Loosen clothing
- Observe the victim closely, noting what the victim was doing when the seizure occurred, the duration of the seizure and other distinct activity that can be reported to the healthcare provider.
- Call 9-1-1 or local emergency services if any of the following apply:
- You are not familiar with the victim's medical history
- The seizure activity persists for longer than five minutes

- Another seizure occurs

DON'T:

- Restrain the victim
- Place anything in the victim's mouth
- Leave the victim by him- or herself

Fainting

If you or anyone you are with begin to feel faint, you should sit down on the closest chair or the floor if necessary and place your head between your knees. If dizziness or fainting is a recurrent issue, immediately contact your healthcare provider. Do not attempt to drive. Call 9-1-1 or local emergency services if you are alone, as it may be indicative of an underlying medical condition.

If you witness someone faint, position him or her on their back and place them in the Trendelenburg position if possible. Assess the environment to ensure the victim's and your own safety. If the victim does not regain consciousness, call 9-1-1 or local emergency services and follow the ABC's of CPR.

Minor Skin Alterations

Minor skin alterations such as small cuts and scrapes typically do not require emergency medical attention. However, to prevent infection, it is very important that you have the knowledge and understanding of how to effectively care for them. The following are a few key things to do when caring for a minor skin alteration:

- Stop the bleeding. For minor skin alterations such as a paper cut, bleeding usually subsides on its own. However, if it does not, apply pressure to the alteration with a tissue or gauze pad. Apply pressure for three to five minutes or until bleeding subsides.
- Cleanse the wound. Rinse the skin alteration under cool water and pat dry. You do not need to use soap, as it may be irritating to the wound.

- Apply antiseptic ointment to the skin alteration. You can use a cotton-tipped swab to do so. It is important to avoid applying too much ointment, as it can irritate the surrounding skin. Only apply enough to cover the alteration.
- Apply a band-aid. Though application of a band-aid seems to be a pretty straightforward process, there a few things people often do not consider. Remember, the goal is to prevent infection. Band-aids are considered sterile before you open the protective wrapper. Once the wrapper is open, you will notice one side of the band-aid has paper protecting the gauze pad and adhesive. On the paper side there will be two folds at the center protecting the gauze pad that will cover the wound. Pinch the two folds and carefully pull them away from the center, avoiding contamination of the gauze pad. Once the folds are pulled back and the gauze pad is exposed to air, immediately cover the wound with the gauze pad. Once the wound is covered, pull back the rest of the paper to uncover the remainder of the adhesive. Easy enough, right!

Continue to monitor the minor skin alteration daily. It is important to change the bandage at least once a day or whenever the bandage appears soiled. Continue to keep the skin alteration covered until a pink, beefy tissue covers the wound, which means that infection is no longer a threat. Contact your healthcare provider if you notice signs of infection. The acronym SWEEP can help you identify such signs.

- Swelling
- Warmth
- Erythema (redness)
- Exudation (drainage, especially if an opaque color with a foul odor)
- Pain (increasing in intensity)

Sprained Ligament

A sprain is characterized by any injury to a ligament, the elastic-like bands that connect bones and joints. The most common symptoms observed with a sprain are considerable pain and swelling. If a sprained ligament is suspected, remembering the acronym RICE will assist you in providing prompt and effective care.

- **R**est the affected area. The victim should avoid putting weight on or using the sprained ligament. Splinting or the use of crutches are effective methods to rest and protect the sprained ligament.
- **I**ce. Apply ice to the affected area to reduce swelling and pain. Ice is effective when applied immediately after the injury has occurred. Cover the affected area with a towel or cloth and apply ice. Keep ice on the affected area for 15 to 20 minutes, four to five times daily for the first 48 hours after injury. **NEVER** apply ice directly to your skin or keep ice on an area for more than 20 minutes at a time, as it may cause tissue damage. Initially you reduce the swelling by using ice and after 48 hours or when swelling has subsided, heat may be applied. Use the same rules of thumb (time on and off, not applying directly to skin) for heat application as you would for ice.
- **C**ompress. Ace or elastic bandages can be used to effectively compress the affected area. Compression also assists with reducing swelling. The longer swelling is prevalent, the longer healing time will likely be. When applying a compression bandage, monitor the area for numbness, redness, or increased pain, as this may mean that the bandage is too tight. Provide rest periods for the area by removing the compression bandage. Some compression bandages can be left on for athletics, training and/or occupational activities. Others may need to be removed every 30 minutes. Make sure to read the instructions before applying a compression bandage.
- **E**levate the affected area to promote blood return and

assist in reduction of swelling. Whenever possible, elevate the affected area above the heart.

Non-steroidal anti-inflammatory analgesics (NSAIDs) such as Tylenol or Ibuprofen can be used as an additional measure to reduce pain and inflammation. Avoid too potent of an analgesic as it may mask the pain and impede your ability to prevent further injury.

Sprains are usually resolved in two to three days with the RICE regimen. However, if pain does not subside, or it becomes more painful to apply weight to the affected area, or you develop a fever (> 100 F), you should contact your healthcare provider, as damage to the ligament may be more extensive than you thought.

Fractures

Fractured or broken bones are always considered a medical emergency. If a fracture is suspected, call 9-1-1 or your local emergency services. While waiting for emergency personnel to arrive, complete the following steps to prevent further injury or internal damage. For care of a fracture, remember the acronym ACTION.

- Assess the area to ensure that both you and the victim are free from danger. If you suspect that the situation is dangerous, immediately move to a safe area. If no danger is suspected, avoid moving the victim.
- Compress to stop any bleeding. Bleeding may or may not be present. Bleeding usually occurs if the bone has penetrated through the skin. Apply pressure with a compression bandage, a towel, or an article of clothing. Keep the area sterile if possible. However, in most emergency situations you may not have the supplies or the proper environment to do so.
- Treat the fracture. While waiting for emergency personnel to arrive, the best way to treat the fracture and prevent further injury is immobilizing the affected area. Splinting above and below the injured area is the most effective way to immobilize the fracture. However, do not attempt

to splint the fracture if you are not trained on how to effectively do so, or if it is a neck or spinal cord injury. If a neck or spinal cord injury is suspected **NEVER** move the victim. If you have not been trained on how to use a splint, try to keep the victim calm and instruct him or her to avoid moving the fractured area.

- <u>I</u>ce the area. Same principles apply for fractures as for sprains.
- <u>O</u>bserve for signs of a worsening condition. Signs of a worsening condition include sudden loss of consciousness, hemorrhage, or shock. If the victim becomes unconscious, apply the ABCs of CPR to stabilize him or her. If hemorrhaging occurs, continue to apply pressure until emergency personnel arrive. Signs that indicate shock include feelings of faintness, shortness of breath, vomiting, and/or changes in pupil size (usually dilated). If these signs become apparent, place the victim in the Trendelenburg position (discussed above in the CPR section) if possible.
- <u>N</u>ever leave the victim alone!

Concussion

A concussion is the most common type of head injury. Individuals who engage in contact sports are the most susceptible to concussion and may not notice when one occurs. Some of the common signs of a concussion include headache, confusion, short lapses in consciousness, and memory loss of the event in which the concussion occurred. Contact a healthcare provider if a concussion is suspected so that the extent of damage can be evaluated. If you suspect a child has a head injury, always contact a healthcare provider for further evaluation.

Some symptoms of a concussion may not occur until two weeks to two months after the injury. These symptoms include, but are not limited to, sleep disturbances, irritability, and altered concentration. If any symptoms arise that affect your ability to complete activities of daily living (ADL's), contact your healthcare provider.

Seek medical advice if any of the following symptoms arise, as they may indicate a severe head injury:

- Prolonged headache or dizziness
- Vision or eye disturbances, including pupils that are dilated or of unequal sizes
- Nausea or vomiting
- Impaired balance
- Prolonged memory loss
- Ringing in the ears
- Loss of smell or taste
- Drainage from the ears (bleeding or clear cerebrospinal fluid)
- Bruising around the eyes (Raccoon eyes)

The latest medical advice for teens and children is for them to rest longer than adults after a concussion. A brain injury simply heals more slowly for them. Major League Baseball (MLB), for one, recently instituted a policy of an automatic seven-day disabled list stay for a player who suffers a concussion. However, this is not a policy that youth coaches should copy automatically. **Each player who suffers a concussion should be evaluated individually for the timing of his or her return.**

Food Poisoning

Young players eat before, after and often during games, which can lead to stomach sickness and upset that can be mistaken for other, more serious conditions. It is important for a coach to have a general idea of how to distinguish food poisoning from just a player sick from junk food.

Food poisoning may occur from ingestion of contaminated, undercooked, or expired food or fluids. Some common symptoms of food poisoning include:

- Nausea and vomiting
- Diarrhea

- Fever (>100 F)
- Pallor (pale-colored skin)
- Abdominal pain and discomfort

If a player develops food poisoning, the best treatment is rest and adequate fluids. As with gastroenteritis and most GI alteration, it is crucial that you prevent dehydration. Also, avoid the use of anti-diarrheal medications such as Imodium, as you want to allow the body to excrete the ingested toxins. Food poisoning can develop within hours of ingesting contaminated food or fluids and can persist from days to weeks.

Advise the player and/or parents to contact their healthcare provider if they notice bloody stools, persistent vomiting and/or diarrhea (> two to three days), uncontrolled fever, or if dehydration occurs.

Appendicitis

Appendicitis occurs when the appendix becomes inflamed and filled with mucous from the GI tract. It is important to understand the signs and symptoms of appendicitis to prevent further inflammation and mucous accumulation, which will essentially lead to rupture of the appendix. Prompt medical attention and removal of the appendix (appendectomy) before it ruptures will prevent complications such as peritonitis (infection of the peritoneum) or sepsis (widespread infection). Signs and symptoms of appendicitis are generally associated with the lower right quadrant of your abdomen and include:

- Pain around the navel that shifts to the right lower quadrant of the abdomen (pain increases as the appendix becomes more inflamed)
- Rebound tenderness of the right lower quadrant of the abdomen (when you push in on the abdomen and quickly release, sharp pain occurs upon release)
- Nausea and vomiting
- Fever
- Constipation

It is recommended that you review this section on First Aid prior to the start of the season each year and at least once during the season. This is for your safety as well as for the safety of the players for whom you are responsible.

How to seek outside help

As stated above, if you are in doubt in any situation, seek outside help. It is important to remember that before making any accusations or speaking with parents, make sure you have thoughtfully evaluated the situation and sought a second opinion. This being said, don't feel intimidated when a child is in need. When seeking outside help it is important to get recommendations from people you trust who have had success with live helpers (not someone you found on Google or other impersonal means), such as counselors, therapists, private coaches, doctors, etc. Personal recommendations are often the best way to get the right help. The written materials and website resources listed below are the best guides available at the time of this book's publication.

Resources:

Child Abuse:

Your local state has a child welfare agency with a hotline to report abuse. For example, in Illinois it is 1-800-25Abuse.

Substance Abuse Information and Services (Including Steroids):

-The Hazeldon Foundation and Clinic
www.Hazeldon.com
1-800-257-7800

-SAMSHA
The Substance Abuse and Mental Health Services Administration
A Federal agency that publishes solid information on substance abuse and mental illness.
www.SAMHSA.gov
1-877-SAMSA7

General Resources:
The International Sports Professionals Association (ISPA)
www.TheSportsProfessionals.com
312-920-9522
Certified Sports Professionals in all fields to help and consult.
Programs and information on sports aids.

Bullying and Teasing:
Noggin Power 2 Publication
www.NogginPower2.com
Guides on how to prevent and intervene to stop bullying and teasing.
Other parenting guides as well, such as sleeping help, discipline,
etc.

First Aid:
American Red Cross
www.RedCross.org

Therapists and Counselors:
www.therapists.psychologytoday.com
One of the better sites where you can see the personality and style of
individual therapists.

American Psychological Association (APA)
www.apa.org

National Register of Healthcare Providers in Psychology
www.NationalRegister.org

Legal Issues
The most important things you can do to protect yourself legally
is operating within the scope of your expertise and having liability
insurance. You will most likely have liability insurance through the
league or coaching body you are a part of. If you are unsure of your
coverage, contact your league or governing body. It is important that
you have liability insurance in case of an unforeseen event. Numerous

times throughout this book it has been made clear that if you are unsure of something, seek help. If you are not a doctor, do not attempt to treat a serious injury. If you are not a physical therapist, do not attempt to rehab a damaged shoulder. I think you see where this is going. As a sports coach you are instructing players in the proper way to play a sport and through the EYC Coaching Model you are also promoting critical developmental skills. As long as you stick to this level of instruction you will be operating within the scope of your expertise and should not encounter any legal issues.

Keywords:
Bullying
Teasing
Power Tools
Drugs
Alcohol
Physical/Sexual Abuse
First Aid Kit
Heimlich Maneuver
CPR
AED
Heart Attack
Anaphylaxis
Seizures
Fainting
Sprained Ligament
Fractures
Concussion
Appendicitis

Questions:
1) (True or False) Studies have shown that over 50% of adolescents bully others.
2) Why is it important that we stop bullying?
3) List three tactics of bullies.
4) (True or False) Most bullying takes place in activities such as sports.

5) List three common goals of bullying.
6) List three strategies for eliminating bullying.
7) What is the #1 drug problem in the USA?
8) (True or False) Youth coaches don't have to worry about drug use.
9) List three actions/ behaviors that may indicate a drug problem.
10) (True or False) Many coaches are <u>not</u> mandated to report sexual abuse in the state where they coach.
11) List five items that every well-stocked First Aid Kit contains.
12) When should you dial 9-1-1?
13) List five signs of a severe head injury.
14) What are the two most important things you can do to protect yourself legally while coaching?

Suggested Activities:
1) Create your own First Aid Kit for coaching purposes.

Chapter 14
Dealing With Parents

One of the greatest sources of stress and anxiety a coach can encounter is dealing with players' parents. For the most part this stress and anxiety is more a product of coaches' imagination and media sensationalism. However, there are genuine issues that arise when dealing with parents, and an EYC coach must be prepared to handle these issues in a thoughtful manner. Many of the issues that arise when dealing with parents are the product of a coach who is either dismissive or ineffective at communicating with them. This chapter will help you avoid being a coach who deals ineffectively with parents. Some issues arise that are outside of a coach's control. This typically happens when parents allow their personality to invade your team. This chapter will help you deal with these situations and many more. Before we continue on it is important to understand that parents do have an important role on the team and as a coach you must recognize this importance by always keeping an open line of communication with them. This chapter will bring two different perspectives into the fold, both a player's perspective and a parent's perspective. The player's perspective will help you understand how your players view their parent's role in their sports participation. The parent's perspective will help you understand the expectations of the players' parents. These perspectives will supply a coach with the necessary insights to effectively deal with parents. By employing the insights offered in this chapter a coach will be able to focus more on their team because they will not have the distractions of dealing with unruly parents.

Before we take a look at the two perspectives, let's first define the role parents play in youth sports. Please note, this list is not meant to be exhaustive but rather give coaches a general idea of a parent's role in youth sports.

Parents' Role
-Support
    *Mental
    *Emotional
    *Financial
-Transportation
-Fan base
-Nutrition
-First Aid
-Dry Cleaning (not true for all players)

An Introduction from a Player's Perspective

A player's loyalty rests in two camps. Camp one is your parents, who play a tremendous role in your life. You only have to look at the "Parents' Role" list above to see the enormous role parents play in their child's sporting career. With all the involvement that parents have in their child's sporting endeavors it is quite common for players to go out of their way to "impress" their parents. There will be more discussion shortly about this drive to impress parents, but for now it suffices to say that most youth athletes' primary loyalty rests in their parents' camp.

The second camp a player's loyalty lies with is their coach. As an EYC coach you gain this loyalty through respect, not through intimidation. Players are constantly evaluating a coach's opinion of them. Even the subtlest things you do as a coach can potentially give off signs to your players even if nothing is intended. Players will also notice how you interact with their parents. A coach who acts dismissively toward parents shows a lack of commitment to the team as a whole. A coach who is aggressive toward the parents is creating an awkward environment, because ultimately the player's loyalty is with their parents. A player who sees his or her coach openly and effectively communicating with parents not only feels good about their parents being treated well but also sees a respectful adult relationship. By observing this relationship players have a chance to see how mature adults act in an environment outside of their home. This observation can have tremendous impact on how a player will interact with people throughout their lives.

Another benefit of keeping an open line of communication with parents is that it takes some of the "burden" off of players for describing details of the team. While most children are more than happy to talk about what they themselves did during practices and games, oftentimes they are less excited to talk about "what coach said" or what other players did. However, parents often like to hear about the whole team after they have heard their child's personal stories. Oftentimes children are tired after practices and games, and after they have finished with their personal stories they just want to sit back and relax. A parent who bombards a player with questions can cause him or her to get irritable (very common during the teenage years). A coach who keeps parents up to date on the team is limiting the "what did coach say" questions and allowing players a much needed break after practices and games.

Ultimately your loyalty as a coach is to your players. However, by keeping an open line of communication with players' parents you are alleviating one possible source of stress in the players' lives. By removing sources of stress you are maximizing their potential to perform at their best. Please refer back to Chapter Two for strategies on how to effectively communicate as a coach, as this will help you when talking to parents.

Parents' Perspective

Your relationship with the parents of the players on your team is one of the most challenging aspects of coaching young people. Quite frankly, how you relate to parents can make or break your success as a coach. And we're not just talking here about peewees. You will encounter strenuous challenges from the parents of players at all levels of sports participation, even through to the ranks of professional athletes.

There are a wide variety of parent types that you will encounter in your coaching career, no matter how short or long that career lasts. The range of these types of parents spans from those who are totally uninvolved to the point that you never see them, to those who are so over-involved and controlling that they believe they know how to coach better than you, and they constantly remind you of this. These parents will communicate their purportedly superior knowledge in direct and indirect (behind your back) ways.

Let's address these two extreme groups of parents first. The **absentee parents** may appear at first to be every coach's dream, but there are many pitfalls to working with the children of these parents. The younger the player, the more you will need contact with the player's parents to enable the child's participation in the sport. Most sports leagues will require parents to at least register the player, pay for registration and participate in fundraising for the team and/or league, as well as take a turn performing certain duties with other parents on the team such as providing refreshments, cleaning the playing field or court, taking care of team equipment and so forth. Absentee parents obviously undermine the spirit of the team by not doing their share of these duties. Parents who do participate may complain at home about the parents who do not pull their weight. The effects on team unity can be poisonous. Retribution against the player for the actions of their parents may be meted out on the playing field, and bullying and teasing may occur. These scenarios undermine everything you are trying to accomplish as a coach, and you may have no idea why team chemistry is falling apart. It is all happening out of range of your eyes and ears. Teamwork is compromised and your success is lost.

On one team we were involved with, one of the players had skills far and above the rest of the players. This player had absentee parents. At the beginning of the season this player's exceptional skills were embraced by his teammates and team unity was high. However, the player's parents were never seen and their turns at cleaning uniforms, providing snacks and other shared duties went unattended. As the season went on the players gradually distanced themselves from the exceptional player. He wasn't invited to get-togethers the other teammates held and he was isolated in practices. Eventually the other players started not to feed him the ball at games and the team began to lose. Moreover, the whole team looked depressed, like they weren't having fun. Only near the end of the season did the coach overhear some parents gossiping about the exceptional player's home life, with snide remarks like "there must be something wrong with that kid." The coach realized that his star player was being ostracized because his parents never participated. The season was a disappointment. Later we heard that the player had quit the sport because he was so disenchanted.

Parents who are over-involved can sabotage the team just as much as absentee parents. It is tempting to view these parents positively, seeing them as exceptionally helpful, generous people whose aim is to help the team with everything they have. However, their generosity has to be considered in light of what the other parents are capable of giving as well. Coaches commonly take such generous parents to be a dream come true, but there are negatives. The parents who cannot help with the same resources as the overly generous parents may become jealous and vent their feelings on the players or the team. Again, team harmony is compromised and your success is diminished.

Next consider the **over-involved parents** who meddle with your coaching decisions, try to exert their knowledge or influence over you, are loud and abusive to you, and inevitably break the rules you set down for the team. These parents certainly don't act from a place of heartfelt generosity as above, and typically have their own unresolved issues with sports, or coaches or the school or league you are coaching in. They are negative, and their effect on the players and the success of the team is poisonous. Some coaches believe that the solution to handling these overly involved parents follows the old axiom, *hold your friends close and your enemies closer.* These coaches try to befriend the negative parents and even give them important roles on the team. The coach may even make them assistant coaches. All of these maneuvers are attempts to quell these parents' negativity. These techniques may seem to work in the short term, but over the course of the season they will fail for a number of reasons. The most common reason is that these people can never be satisfied and their negativity will show up somehow in their involvement with the team.

The most successful way to handle both extremes of parents is by insisting on the same winning formula for all the parents of the players on your team. It is important that you establish strong and frequent communication with all parents, orientating them to your coaching style, expectations, rules and techniques early and often. Keep consistent with your team rules, and establish that all parent participation should be equal and balanced, with no parent doing more or less than any other (to the extent that it's within your power to exercise such control over these fellow adults). If one adult does more for the team than the others, they must be stopped, and any resource they provide returned. Do this consistently and demonstratively so the rest of the parents get the message that they are all equal on the team. If you follow these principles, you will be able to handle most parent situations – the two extremes mentioned above and everything in between.

Be careful of how insidiously problems can start with team parents. Allowing certain parents to be on the sidelines with the players, not speaking up when a parent shows up with handfuls of fantastic treats for the team, and not stopping a parent from volunteering comments about what they observed in the game during your post-game wrap-up are all subtle ways in which parents compromise your control over the team. Stop such actions early in the season.

Several of the techniques mentioned above deserve further elaboration. **Orientation** is a prime example. Many coaches gather parents at the beginning of the season for a "parents' meeting." Most often the coach does this just because he or she has been told to do it. When a coach doesn't recognize the importance of an orientation meeting, such meetings frequently deteriorate into excuses for adult drinking parties with little team information exchanged. Your initial team meeting sets a tone for how parents will view you from that day forward. Done poorly, a parent orientation meeting can be the catalyst for the extreme parent groups to manifest themselves. Your role at the parents' meeting is to conduct business, not to entertain. It would be great to do this within the context of everyone having fun, but having fun is not your prime objective. You need to give parents a taste of who you are as a coach, explain your style and philosophy of coaching, go through the rules and expectations for the players and their parents and to build enthusiasm for the upcoming season. This should all be conveyed in a style that shows you are in command of the meeting, as distinct from the party atmosphere mentioned earlier, with your business agenda getting shoved aside to the "by-the-way" moment. A good way to structure the meeting is to have a clear separation between its "business" portion and any "social" aspect you may plan. Introduce yourself, walk the parents through your rules and expectations, share your vision for the season and then have the refreshments and the social hour. Your season will be smoother if you lead the meeting authoritatively. Another mistake is to hold only one parent meeting during the season. It may seem like a burden to hold several parent meetings throughout the season, but we assure you that your coaching job will be much easier if you do. We should emphasize that we are talking about players at all levels. Coaches of older players are particularly negligent in keeping parents involved in and informed about the team. This is a catastrophic mistake.

Another technique that deserves to be highlighted here is the announcement and explanation of **team rules**. Earlier discussions in this book have discussed setting team rules. The thing to emphasize here is that parents have a key role in your enforcement of rules. Leaving parents out of the orientation to these rules and not including some guidelines for parent behavior itself is dangerous to your success. And, again, we emphasize, this is vital for coaching players of all ages.

Another essential technique in dealing with parents is **consistency**. Nothing fires up the wrath of parents more than for you to be inconsistent in how you handle the players on your team. Some coaches fly by the seat of their pants when it comes to enforcing team rules. They make decisions on the spot and these decisions turn out to be different each time they are made. Your rules should be solid guideposts for handling player/parent situations. It is important to refer back to them even in situations that seem to demand immediate attention. Many coaches get themselves into traps by making decisions in the moment and get caught up in immediate success rather than focusing on the long-term goals of the season and program success. It is here where your team rules are your best friend. You crafted them intelligently. Rely on them and trust in them.

These essential skills – COMMUNICATION, ORIENTATION, RULE SETTING and CONSISTENCY – along with the broader theme of this manual, ETHICS IN COACHING, which assumes

FAIRNESS and MUTUAL RESPECT, all fall under the definition of a larger skill essential for a coach, which is:

LEADERSHIP

Being a leader for your players and parents must involve these essential skills. The very definition of leadership demands two other essential skills as well. These are **COURAGE** and **DECISION MAKING**. It takes courage to face young athletes and teach them a sport. A leader must be able and willing to make decisions and stick with them. This can also be called *decisiveness*.

Our discussion above may seem complex, but breaking down the larger concept of leadership into these essential skills actually makes them simpler for a coach to embrace and use. Build these skills into your coaching and you will be a strong leader of the players and the parents.

Make note of the many valuable skills that are <u>not</u> highlighted here. Such skills as strategy, humor, inspiration, forcefulness, etc. are not included in our essentials of leadership.

The essential skills of strong leadership are: Communication, Orientation, Mutual Respect, Rule-Setting, Consistency, Courage, Decision-Making/Decisiveness, Ethics, and Fairness.

All this being said, what are parents looking for in the coaches who care for their children? Certainly most parents would not argue that these essential skills of leadership are all aspects of a coach they want for their child/young adult. And yet, certainly, parents want their children to learn and become better at sports, as that is one of the main reasons why they have introduced them to the sport.

Certainly, parents want their child to learn and become more proficient at a sport.

We could elaborate on many other personality qualities that parents want to see in their child's coach. To keep things simple, we can sum up most of these by stating: *Parents want their children treated in the way they <u>ideally</u> treat their children.* We say ideally because one of the landmines a coach can step on with parents is that the coach sees parents yelling at their children or parents being aggressive with their children and the coach automatically assumes that parents will condone the coach using the same techniques. This is a huge mistake. Parents want you to care for their children in the way they perceive they act toward them. So many parents who are yellers or who are otherwise aggressive with their children <u>do not</u> see themselves as such. And they do not want you to be aggressive with their children.

Thus, in terms of your personality and approach, yelling at players is wrong. Maybe more importantly, yelling and an aggressive manner are simply not effective, particularly with today's athletes. The minute you yell at players, just like any human being in any situation, their natural defenses will consume them and they will not listen to your instruction. Now, there are times when you have to raise your voice over the din of the game or practice, but this is not "yelling" in the same sense as demeaning the person or attempting to gain power over the person through your communication. The more effective manner to adopt is one in which you are businesslike in your approach, tone of voice, and emotional expression toward players. Think about this carefully – you wouldn't expect to get an adult co-worker to respond to a request by using strong, abusive language. Why would that be successful with a younger person?

Another landmine that coaches step on is anger toward players. Like some parents, coaches get angry with young people when they fail to accomplish tasks and/or fail to live up to expectations. You have to ask yourself, why do some coaches get angry? Young people are not finished products. Are they supposed to behave exactly like we do? Coaches often ask a young person to perform a feat that they cannot do and maybe never will be able to do in their athletic career. How can we get mad at them? Anger has no place in coaching. Frustration maybe, but not anger.

Anger has no place in coaching young people.

Parents want coaches to keep their children safe, teach them the sport, treat them well and to enable them to have fun.

Lastly, many coaches have a habit of referring to the players on their team as "my kids" or even "my little babies" or some other term that conveys a closer relationship than coach and player. Be careful of referring to the players in a manner that muddles just whose kids they are. When a coach takes that stance of OWNERSHIP with their players they are traveling down a slippery slope of inevitable loss and hurt feelings. It is important to know your role in the lives of these kids. This role is limited. You are in these players' lives for a short time. Coaches have always been and always will be a strong influence on the lives of young people. The perspective suggested here of knowing your role doesn't diminish that strong influence. Knowing your role in the lives of these players and staying within that role is an invaluable perspective that can help a coach cope with the often-strenuous task of coaching young people.

To be in the lives of young people, even for a short time, is an honor. You are there for them, not they for you.

In closing, as you think about your role with the parents of the players, it probably will come as no surprise to realize that coaches today at all levels need to be diplomats toward parents associated with your team as well as the general public. This diplomacy requires your communication skills to be savvy, and to be something you work at as much as your X's and O's. Not convinced? Just think about the professional and college coaches you see in the media and consider how essential it is for them to make comments and be available for interviews after games, and to appear on TV shows or comment for news articles between games. See how they handle all this extra work beyond the coaching? The best of them know that this is part of coaching today, and they work at it as much as their other coaching skills. No matter what level you coach at, this same dynamic will filter down to your level of coaching. Handling parents of peewees is very comparable to the pro coach being interviewed by the media. In fact, if you have any ambition of moving up in the coaching ranks you can hone your media handling skills by practicing your diplomacy and leadership with parents no matter what the level of the sport.

Reflections

How you deal with parents is critical to your success as a coach. While there are certain difficulties in dealing with parents, overall it need not be a difficult process. Most parents are concerned primarily about their child being in good hands and succeeding. By being an EYC coach you are ensuring parents that their children are safe and by keeping an open line of communication you are keeping parents up to date on their child's progress. As an EYC coach you have taken the steps necessary to deal effectively with parents and ensure that your players can participate in the most distraction-free environment possible. When you encounter difficult situations with parents review this chapter for guidance and go over your EYC Coach Checklist to ensure that you are conducting yourself in a manner consistent with EYC coaching principles. Once you are assured of the soundness of your coaching and that you have done everything in your power to handle the difficult situation don't stress out if certain parents still do not respond favorably. The age-old adage applies perfectly to dealing with parents: "You can't please everyone." Oftentimes well-intentioned coaches try to please parents by making exceptions and, as a result, a snowball effect of exceptions begin and ultimately you are left with a bunch of unhappy parents. As was mentioned earlier, you must be a leader as a coach and be willing to stand firm on your principles. At the end of the day being an EYC coach means standing up for your coaching principles and being able to defend them in the face of adversity.

Keywords:
Absentee Parents
Over-Involved Parents
Orientation
Team Rules
Consistency

Courage
Decision-Making

Study Questions:

1) (True or False) Most of a coach's anxiety when it comes to dealing with parents is overblown.
2) (True or False) Parents have an important role on the team.
3) List three roles that parents have in their child's sporting career.
4) In which two camps does a player's loyalty rest?
5) What are two advantages to effectively communicating with parents?
6) (True or False) How you interact with parents cannot effect your coaching.
7) (True or False) The younger the player, the more contact you will have with their parents.
8) Describe some of the negative aspects of parental over-involvement.
9) Why is consistency so important when dealing with parents?
10) List the essential skills of strong leadership.

Appendix A
The Plan in Action

The following is a sample plan for a boy's little league team summer season. This sample plan is meant to show how you can implement the five stages of player development into the season. The bullet point below each stage is the primary focus during this stage.

Pre-season meeting: May 28 (Stage 1) **Laying the Foundation**
-Establish team rules.

Practice: 1-4. May 30-June 6 (Stage 2) **Building the Frame**
-Focus on team as a whole.

Practice: 5-6. June 7-10 (Stage 3) **Exterior Finishes**
-More emphasis on individual skill development while keeping focus on team.

Games: 1-18. June 11- August 8 (Stage 4) **Working on the Interior**
-Focus on sportsmanship and utilize the winning factor.

End of Season: Party August 20 (Stage 5) **Laying the Field**
-Congratulate players on a great season.

Appendix B
Playing Time Template

The following is the essential information that you will need to help determine playing time and how to utilize various lineups on your team. Due to the varying time lengths and dynamics of the various team sports, a template has not been provided to determine your teams lineups throughout the game.

Winning Factor
5-7yrs: 10%
8-11yrs: 20%
12-14yrs: 40%
15-18yrs: 60%

Player Levels
High Talent (HT)
Above Average Talent (AAT)
Average Talent (AT)
Below Average Talent (BAT)

Team Winning Factor: _____ (i.e. 10%)

Length of game: _____ X Winning Factor: _____
(i.e., 30 minutes X .20 = 6 minutes to focus on winning. Therefore, for 24 minutes your focus is on allowing the whole team to play and not solely on winning)

Time for Maximum Lineup (number from above equation): _____

Time for Alternate Lineup: _____

Appendix C
Additional Helpful Resources

Moms Team

http://www.momsteam.com

A website developed from a parent's perspective. However, it also has a lot to offer coaches. The information provided on this website is compiled from highly qualified individuals and addresses a wide variety of topics.

Coaches Choice

http://www.coacheschoice.com

Coaches Choice is one of the leading publishers of sports-specific books. Coaches looking to expand their knowledge base will find many great options here.

Sideline Sports Doc

http://sidelinesportsdoc.com

A great program for coaches looking to increase their understanding of sports injuries and how to treat them.

American Red Cross

http://www.redcross.org

The American Red Cross is the industry leader in First Aid and CPR. Most states offer sports-specific programs; check with your local chapter to see course offerings.

Noggin Power 2

http://www.nogginpower2.com

Provides outstanding resources for both coaches and parents on a variety of issues that will help in developing the complete player.

The International Sports Professionals Association

http://www.theISPA.org

The International Sports Professionals Association is the leading credentialing body of sports professionals in the world. Provides coaches with a wealth of resources and cutting edge information.

References

Arsenio, W. F., Adams, E., & Gold, J. (2009). Social information processing, moral reasoning, and emotion attributions: Relations with adolescents' reactive and proactive aggression. *Child Development, 80, 1739-1755. doi:10.1111/j.1467-8624.2009.01365.x*

Arsenio, W. F., & Gold, J. (2006*).* The effects of social injustice and inequality on children's moral judgments and behavior: Towards a theoretical model. *Cognitive Development, 21, 388-400. doi:10.1016/j. cogdev.2006.06.005*

Bjork, Robert A.; William B. Whitten (1974). "Recency-Sensitive Retrieval Processes in Long-Term Free Recall". *Cognitive Psychology* **6**: 173-189.

Bright-Paul, Alexandra; Jarrold, Christopher; Wright, Daniel B. (2008). *Developmental Psychology, Vol 44(4), Jul 2008, 1055-1068. doi:* 10.1037/0012-1649.44.4.1055

Briefing Sheet (Mental health): Self-esteem, confidence and adult learning. (n.d.). Retrieved from http://lennyspence.weebly.com/ uploads/2/3/1/7/2317969/self-esteem-confidence.pdf

Davis, Douglas D. (2010). Child Development: A Practitioners Guide. *New York: Guilford. 494 pgs.*

Developing the Whole Player. (n.d.). Retrieved from www. oronohealthyyouth.org/uploads/Coaches.pdf

Ethical Standards | Minor Track Association. (n.d.). Retrieved from http://minortrack.netfirms.com/clubs/ethical-standards/

Examining Strategies Outstanding High School Football Coaches Use to Develop Life Skills and Character in their Payers.(n.d.). Retrieved from http://www.educ.msu.edu/ysi/articles/ NFLCharitiesCoachingLifeSkills.pd

Gräfenhain, M, Behne, T, Carpenter, M, Tomasello. (2009). Developmental Psychology. *Vol 45(5), Sep 2009, 1430-1443. doi:* 10.1037/a0016122

Kall, Robert V. Advances in Child Development and Behavior. *Vol.35 2010. New York: Elsevier*

Maholmes, Valerie, et. al. (2010) Applied Research in Child and Adlescent Development: A Practical Guide. *New York: Taylor & Francis. 340 pgs.*

Mayer, J and Filstead, W. (1984). Adolescence and Alcohol. *New York: Ballinger*

Mayer, J. (1989). The Adolescent Alcohol Involvement Scale-*AAIS*.

Mayer, J. (2009) Family Fit. *Chicago: NP2/ISPA Pub.*

Modeling Appropriate Behavior. (n.d.). Retrieved from http:// www.childsharing.com/ResourceCenter/Articles/Parenting/ Modeling-Appropriate-Behavior.doc

Piaget, J. (1981). Intelligence and affectivity: Their relationship during child development *(T. Brown & C. Kaegi, Trans.). Palo Alto, CA: Annual Reviews.*

Posner, M, Rothbart, M. (2007). Educating the human brain. *Washington, DC, US: American Psychological Association. (2007). xiii, 263 pp. doi:* 10.1037/11519-000

Rudd, A, & Stoll, S. (1997). What type of character do athletes possess?. *The Sport Journal, 7*(2), Retrieved from http://www. thesportjournal.org doi: 1543-9518

Santrock, John M. (2010) Child Development. The 40 Developmental Assets. *New York: McGraw-Hill. 648 pgs. Search Institute Minneapolis, MN.*

Smith, C., Cudaback, D., Goddard, H.W., & Myers-Walls, J. (1994). National Extension Parent Education Model of Critical Parenting Practices. *Retrieved from* http://www.cyfernet.org/parenting_ practices/preface.html

Youth Sports in America: An Overview. (n.d.). Retrieved from

http://www.fitness.gov/youthsports.pdf

Youth Sport Coaching: Development, Approaches, and Educational Needs. (n.d.). Retrieved from http://www.educ.msu.edu/ysi/ project/CriticalIssuesYouthSports.pdf